Listen, Lord

REV. FRANCIS R. DAVIS
ST. PATRICK'S CHURCH
274 DENISON PKWY. E.
CORNING, NEW YORK 14830-2995

Listen, Lord

Short Reflections and Simple Prayers
Based on the Sunday Readings

Rev. Walter J. Paulits

Nihil Obstat
>Rev. Hilarion Kistner, O.F.M.
>Rev. Lawrence J. Mick

Imprimi Potest
>Rev. Norman Perry, O.F.M.
>Vicar Provincial

Imprimatur
>+Daniel E. Pilarczyk, V.G.
>Archdiocese of Cincinnati
>May 31, 1979

The *Nihil Obstat* and *Imprimatur* are a declaration that a book or pamphlet is considered to be free from doctrinal or moral error. It is not implied that those who have granted the *Nihil Obstat* and *Imprimatur* agree with the contents, opinions or statements expressed.

Scripture texts used in this work are taken from the *New American Bible*, copyright ©1970 by the Confraternity of Christian Doctrine, Washington, D.C., and are used by permission of copyright owner. All rights reserved.

Cover and book design by Julie Van Leeuwen.

SBN 0-912228-63-6

©1979 St. Anthony Messenger Press
All rights reserved.
Printed in the U.S.A.

Dedication

To my family: Mom, Pop, John and Irene, Matt and Loretta, Marie and Harry and all the children—a great group in which to learn what the family of God must be all about!

Acknowledgements

I express my deep appreciation to the parishioners of St. John, Westminster, for their encouragement as I wrote these meditations; to my family, who have shown an unflagging interest in its progress; to Mr. Timothy Dunn, who suggested my manuscript to its present editor and publisher; to Mrs. Brenda Rote, who did some of the typing; and to my editors, Father Jeremy Harrington, O.F.M., for his kind cooperation and suggestions, and Father Greg Friedman, O.F.M., and Ms. Carol Luebering, for their ingenious editing of my basic texts.

Table of Contents

Cycle A

Advent Season	1
Christmas Season	5
Lenten Season	12
Easter Season	19
Trinity Sunday	29
Corpus Christi	30
Season of the Year	31

Cycle B

Advent Season	67
Christmas Season	71
Lenten Season	77
Easter Season	85
Trinity Sunday	93
Corpus Christi	94
Season of the Year	95

Cycle C

Advent Season	129
Christmas Season	133
Lenten Season	139
Easter Season	147
Trinity Sunday	156
Corpus Christi	157
Season of the Year	158

Holydays and Holidays

Immaculate Conception	192
All Saints	193
Assumption	194
Mother's Day	195
Father's Day	196
Thanksgiving	197

TABLE OF SUNDAYS AND MOVABLE FEASTS

Cycle	C	A	B	C	A	B
	1979	1980	1981	1982	1983	1984
1st Sun. of Advent	Dec. 2	Nov. 30	Nov. 29	Nov. 28	Nov. 27	Dec. 2
2nd Sun. of Advent	Dec. 9	Dec. 7	Dec. 6	Dec. 5	Dec. 4	Dec. 9
3rd Sun. of Advent	Dec. 16	Dec. 14	Dec. 13	Dec. 12	Dec. 11	Dec. 16
4th Sun. of Advent	Dec. 23	Dec. 21	Dec. 20	Dec. 19	Dec. 18	Dec. 23
Holy Family	Dec. 30	Dec. 28	Dec. 27	Dec. 26	Dec. 30	Dec. 30
	1980	1981	1982	1983	1984	1985
Epiphany	Jan. 6	Jan. 4	Jan. 3	Jan. 2	Jan. 8	Jan. 6
Baptism of the Lord	Jan. 13	Jan. 11	Jan. 10	Jan. 9	——	Jan. 13
2nd Sun. of the Year	Jan. 20	Jan. 18	Jan. 17	Jan. 16	Jan. 15	Jan. 20
3rd Sun. of the Year	Jan. 27	Jan. 25	Jan. 24	Jan. 23	Jan. 22	Jan. 27
4th Sun. of the Year	Feb. 3	Feb. 1	Jan. 31	Jan. 30	Jan. 29	Feb. 3
5th Sun. of the Year	Feb. 10	Feb. 8	Feb. 7	Feb. 6	Feb. 5	Feb. 10
6th Sun. of the Year	Feb. 17	Feb. 15	Feb. 14	Feb. 13	Feb. 12	Feb. 17
7th Sun. of the Year	——	Feb. 22	Feb. 21	——	Feb. 19	——
8th Sun. of the Year	——	Mar. 1	——	——	Feb. 26	——
9th Sun. of the Year	——	——	——	——	Mar. 4	——
Ash Wednesday	Feb. 20	Mar. 4	Feb. 24	Feb. 16	Mar. 7	Feb. 20
1st Sun. of Lent	Feb. 24	Mar. 8	Feb. 28	Feb. 20	Mar. 11	Feb. 24

Cycle	C 1980	A 1981	B 1982	C 1983	A 1984	B 1985
2nd Sun. of Lent	Mar. 2	Mar. 15	Mar. 7	Feb. 27	Mar. 18	Mar. 3
3rd Sun. of Lent	Mar. 9	Mar. 22	Mar. 14	Mar. 6	Mar. 25	Mar. 10
4th Sun. of Lent	Mar. 16	Mar. 29	Mar. 21	Mar. 13	Apr. 1	Mar. 17
5th Sun. of Lent	Mar. 23	Apr. 5	Mar. 28	Mar. 20	Apr. 8	Mar. 24
Passion Sunday	Mar. 30	Apr. 12	Apr. 4	Mar. 27	Apr. 15	Mar. 31
Easter Sunday	Apr. 6	Apr. 19	Apr. 11	Apr. 3	Apr. 22	Apr. 7
2nd Sun. of Easter	Apr. 13	Apr. 26	Apr. 18	Apr. 10	Apr. 29	Apr. 14
3rd Sun. of Easter	Apr. 20	May 3	Apr. 25	Apr. 17	May 6	Apr. 21
4th Sun. of Easter	Apr. 27	May 10	May 2	Apr. 24	May 13	Apr. 28
5th Sun. of Easter	May 4	May 17	May 9	May 1	May 20	May 5
6th Sun. of Easter	May 11	May 24	May 16	May 8	May 27	May 12
Ascension Thursday	May 15	May 28	May 20	May 12	May 31	May 16
7th Sun. of Easter	May 18	May 31	May 23	May 15	June 3	May 19
Pentecost Sunday	May 25	June 7	May 30	May 22	June 10	May 26
Trinity Sunday	June 1	June 14	June 6	May 29	June 17	June 2
Corpus Christi	June 8	June 21	June 13	June 5	June 24	June 9
10th Sun. of the Year	—	—	—	—	—	—
11th Sun. of the Year	June 15	—	—	June 12	—	June 16
12th Sun. of the Year	June 22	—	June 20	June 19	—	June 23
13th Sun. of the Year	June 29	June 28	June 27	June 26	July 1	June 30
14th Sun. of the Year	July 6	July 5	July 4	July 3	July 8	July 7
15th Sun. of the Year	July 13	July 12	July 11	July 10	July 15	July 14

Cycle	C 1980	A 1981	B 1982	C 1983	A 1984	B 1985
16th Sun. of the Year	July 20	July 19	July 18	July 17	July 22	July 21
17th Sun. of the Year	July 27	July 26	July 25	July 24	July 29	July 28
18th Sun. of the Year	Aug. 3	Aug. 2	Aug. 1	July 31	Aug. 5	Aug. 4
19th Sun. of the Year	Aug. 10	Aug. 9	Aug. 8	Aug. 7	Aug. 12	Aug. 11
20th Sun. of the Year	Aug. 17	Aug. 16	Aug. 15	Aug. 14	Aug. 19	Aug. 18
21st Sun. of the Year	Aug. 24	Aug. 23	Aug. 22	Aug. 21	Aug. 26	Aug. 25
22nd Sun. of the Year	Aug. 31	Aug. 30	Aug. 29	Aug. 28	Sept. 2	Sept. 1
23rd Sun. of the Year	Sept. 7	Sept. 6	Sept. 5	Sept. 4	Sept. 9	Sept. 8
24th Sun. of the Year	Sept. 14	Sept. 13	Sept. 12	Sept. 11	Sept. 16	Sept. 15
25th Sun. of the Year	Sept. 21	Sept. 20	Sept. 19	Sept. 18	Sept. 23	Sept. 22
26th Sun. of the Year	Sept. 28	Sept. 27	Sept. 26	Sept. 25	Sept. 30	Sept. 29
27th Sun. of the Year	Oct. 5	Oct. 4	Oct. 3	Oct. 2	Oct. 7	Oct. 6
28th Sun. of the Year	Oct. 12	Oct. 11	Oct. 10	Oct. 9	Oct. 14	Oct. 13
29th Sun. of the Year	Oct. 19	Oct. 18	Oct. 17	Oct. 16	Oct. 21	Oct. 20
30th Sun. of the Year	Oct. 26	Oct. 25	Oct. 24	Oct. 23	Oct. 28	Oct. 27
31st Sun. of the Year	Nov. 2	Nov. 1	Oct. 31	Oct. 30	Nov. 4	Nov. 3
32nd Sun. of the Year	Nov. 9	Nov. 8	Nov. 7	Nov. 6	Nov. 11	Nov. 10
33rd Sun. of the Year	Nov. 16	Nov. 15	Nov. 14	Nov. 13	Nov. 18	Nov. 17
Christ the King	Nov. 23	Nov. 22	Nov. 21	Nov. 20	Nov. 25	Nov. 24
Mother's Day	May 11	May 10	May 9	May 8	May 13	May 12
Father's Day	June 15	June 21	June 20	June 19	June 17	June 16
Thanksgiving	Nov. 27	Nov. 26	Nov. 25	Nov. 24	Nov. 29	Nov. 28

Introduction

This book grew out of a pastoral need I experienced at St. John's Church, Westminster, Maryland. Our liturgy committee, of which I was chairman, often wanted texts for meditative prayer to be read by a lector after Holy Communion had been distributed and all movement in the sanctuary and the body of the church had ceased. For awhile we used excerpts from various books or occasionally composed a meditation of our own. Finally, for Pentecost Sunday of Cycle C a year or so ago I decided to begin a complete sequence of meditations for every Sunday of the year and for several selected feasts. The parishioners responded beautifully to my first efforts. I was encouraged, and completed the meditations for all three cycles.

The Word of the Lord is always an invitation to dialogue, an opportunity to hear and respond to his voice. And so these prayers begin with the day's readings from Scripture. Basic themes appear and reappear because this is the method employed by the liturgy itself. The "Lord" I address is always Jesus.

I hope these meditations can also be used profitably by individuals preparing for Mass or meditating after Communion or after Mass. I urge that anyone using them allow them to be prayers, and I suggest a simple method of praying them: Place oneself first deeply in the presence of God and then read slowly, reflectively, and with plenty of pauses.

Writing this book has been a theological and spiritual adventure for me. May it be the same for all who read and pray it.

Father Walter J. Paulits
August 31, 1978

Cycle A

Adventure in Newness Is 2:1-5
 Rom 13:11-14
1st Sunday of Advent   A Mt 24:37-44

Today we begin again! No matter what last year was like; no matter how many times we fell flat on our faces in our attempts to be like Christ; no matter how poorly we celebrated the mysteries of his birth, life, death, resurrection and kingship all last year. Today we start a new year. We place everything of last year in his hands and ask him to understand even our maliciousness. For even when we hurt somebody with a kind of cold deliberation, weakness more than devilishness was probably at the heart of what we were doing.

And as for all those real weaknesses—our cowardliness when backbone was asked of us, our stubbornness when forgiveness was needed—all these weaknesses we have confessed. And we say now to the Lord: "Please, never again; they are not the qualities of people whose lives are dead to sin." We know that we will be weak again, but at least let the past be the past. Let his mercy swallow it up. We want to be new again.

Lord, deep within us the Spirit dwells. Deep within our spouses a vibrant and powerful love for us is asking to break forth if we would just listen. Deep within the feast of Christmas is a mystery of life which laughs at death. So why do we live as if the Holy Spirit were not our guest; or as if our spouses can be taken for granted or hurt or put down; or as if Christmas could make sense without celebrating *you*, Lord?

Burn last year's rust away from the crust of our

lives! Turn our eyes inward to our real values and outward to others and to you. Lord, make this Advent an adventure into newness and freshness for us. You are at the heart of all that is, and we are looking for you all during this season. We pray with a voice and heart that echo the deepest wish of the first Christmas: "Come, Lord Jesus!"

An Uncomfortable Presence　　　Is 11:1-10
　　　　　　　　　　　　　　　　　　Rom 15:4-9
2nd Sunday of Advent　A　　　　　　Mt 3:1-12

　　John the Baptizer was probably not the most comfortable man to live with. For one thing he was certainly different: His boyhood had been spent away from normal family influences. He lived alone in the desert for a while. His food was unusual. And his clothing had not been seen around Jerusalem since the days of the great prophets. And what he said was so stern.
　　He was terrifyingly hard on the Pharisees, those who were the most religious and law-abiding people in the land. His warnings to them were brutally clear: "Reform!" But reform from *what*? They obeyed the Law with a scrupulosity that made them revered among the people.
　　John's other warning to them is the clue: not to pride themselves on the claim that Abraham was their ancestor. It is as if John said: "Do not see yourself as sure of God's favor because you happen to be born into his chosen people; do not pride yourself on performing the niceties of the law of the chosen people. For after receiving the favor of a good birth and after having done all that is commanded, you are still unworthy servants. You still need to be reformed."

　　Lord, so many of us were born into the Catholic faith. So many of us have tried to keep the Ten Commandments and the laws of the Church all our lives.

Could John the Baptizer really be speaking to us today? If he is not, it is because we are perfect in our holiness, in our faith, hope and love, in our hatred of all that is evil and selfish, in our desire for everlasting life with you—in other words, it is because we have received all your gifts and have responded to them perfectly.

Honesty makes us shake our heads over that one. No, Lord, we are not perfect. We are not yet like our heavenly Father. John the Baptizer might not be a comfortable person to have around, but his message is vital.

Lord, when John cries out to us, "Reform," help us to begin to remake our lives in your image and likeness.

Shouts of Joy

Is 35:1-6, 10
Jas 5:7-10
Mt 11:2-11

3rd Sunday of Advent   A

Isaiah describes a lovely vision of a desert springing forth into abundant and bursting life. He sees the flowers that will bloom as the desert's shouts of joy. He sees the flat and arid land covered with the cedars that were Lebanon's proud boast. And how will all this happen? Isaiah's words are the key to Advent:

They will see the glory of the LORD,
   the splendor of our God (Is 35:2c).

The same God who spun all that is into beauty and loveliness will restore life and beauty where they have been lost. And only he can do that.

But, of course, Isaiah was not speaking only of the regreening of the Judean deserts. He had something much more important in mind: the strengthening of people who had lost faith in God, the comforting of those who sorrow in exile, the curing of those scarred by evil. The Lord used these same signs to prove to John's followers that he was indeed the one for whom they had been waiting, the signs Isaiah had predicted: sight restored to the blind, mobility to the lame, hearing to the deaf, and enlightenment to those who did not yet know God. And Isaiah adds what the Lord was perhaps too modest to note:

> They will meet with joy and gladness;
> sorrow and mourning will flee (Is 35:10b).

Lord, do we need much more to convince us of the true blessings you came to bring? The Gospel shows you uncomfortable in the presence of sickness and evil; indeed, sometimes your words indicate that you were angry at their presence in the world you had made. Lord, we bless you and thank you for what you came to bring: healing, joy and life without end.

Lord, Christmas is coming. Cure us of all that troubles us; give us the joy of your salvation!

In and Out of the Ordinary

4th Sunday of Advent   A

Is 7:10-14
Rom 1:1-7
Mt 1:18-24

The Gospels offer much evidence of the miraculous surrounding Christ's birth and that of John the Baptizer: the angel which came to Mary and to Elizabeth, Zachary's loss of speech and its sudden return, Joseph's hesitation which the angel resolved, and the songs of angels on Christmas night. These stupendous signs of the power of God in our midst are good for us, and we give thanks for them. They invite us to a faith in a God we cannot see. We are weak, and we sometimes need miracles to snap us back to a realization that God our Father lives and loves and is interested in us.

But miracles are by definition something unusual, something *out* of the ordinary. And most of us live all of our lives very much *in* the ordinary. Something must be good about the ordinary or the Lord would not have given us so much of it. Perhaps we can come to love and value the ordinary which is so much of our lives by pausing to see what was ordinary about Christ's conception and birth. After all, like us he grew for nine months in a woman's womb.

Lord, like us you were born; like us you grew and learned from your mother and father. The miraculous moments in all of this were few; the long days of waiting for birth and the years of growth that followed were ordinary indeed. In other words, Lord, you were as divine in your moment of *human* birth as you were when the Holy Spirit overshadowed Mary. You work in the ordinary as well as in the extraordinary; more, in fact, because there is so much more of it.

Lord, this Christmas let us see you in each other— in our children, in our friends, in the poor and the lonely. They are so ordinary, but they are also you. You said so.

A Birthday Gift of Peace

Is 9:1-6
Ti 2:11-14
Lk 2:1-14

Christmas—Mass at Midnight

What a great and lovely and promise-fulfilled day this is! We celebrate that eternal moment when, in the quiet of the night, all was ready for the Lord to come to live with us. He was to be one of us, to grow in wisdom and age and grace among us, and to enter into a frightening fight with our great enemies—Satan, sin and death. If he had held himself aloof from us, where would we be now? If Father, Son and Spirit had said about us, "They're impossible; forget them," what indeed would our world now be? It's struggle enough with him as our leaven; without him Dachau would be a daily horror.

But Jesus did come. He did choose to empty himself and to become one like us in everything except sin. And because he is what he is, the word that is used so often in the liturgy of this day to describe him is *peace*. The angels sing of peace to the shepherds, and Isaiah's prophecy proclaims the birth of the Lord and the inauguration of a kingdom of justice and peace.

Peace, Lord Jesus, is, as you say, your gift to us; it is a grace. And it seeks our response; all your gifts do. That response, Lord, is a temperate, just, devout, loving and hope-filled life. And we know, Lord, how right that response is, because we know the weariness and ultimate stupidity of sin; we know the shallowness of our lives when you become a stranger; we know the bitterness and folly of letting any kind of passion be our master.
In a word, Lord, we know from our own agony that the world gives no peace. Only you do. It is a great gift, and it begins with your birthday. So, Lord, happy birthday, and thanks!

At the Heart of Our Lives

Sir 3:2-6, 12-14
Col 3:12-21
Mt 2:13-15, 19-23

Sunday in the Octave of Christmas
Holy Family

It is amazing how much of ourselves we have invested in our families. To our wife or our husband we have pledged a love enduring until death. We have left our own fathers and mothers to establish our own homes. The lines of worry and care that we have etched into their faces are being carved into our own, as the love we share as husbands and wives enfleshes itself in our children.
And when the children do come, how complicated and engrossing our original investment becomes! No longer are we only two in one flesh; our oneness multiplies itself, and every human being who becomes a member of the family calls out of our hearts a response of generosity that sometimes has the look of bloody crucifixion about it.
We have learned during our years of family living that we are in a novitiate of unselfishness. We have

learned that our investments are demanding. Sometimes we pull back from the demands; we hesitate to make the sacrifice. We fight and yell and demand our rights. But most of the time we kiss and make up, and the family goes on, strengthened by the stresses it has endured.

Lord Jesus, our family is important to us, and you want it to be. Here are the lives that most touch ours, and the people for whom we most often carry out your command to love as you loved. Here are the persons we know best, Lord, both in their lovableness and in their irritating power to make us want to strangle them. They are the ones, Lord, whose lives we have helped shape. And, Lord, we ought never forget that they have had their part in forming us, too—from the person we married to the baby who taught us to forget about sleeping at two o'clock in the morning.

Our families, Lord, are the heart of our lives. On this feast we ask you, Lord, to bless us and all those you have gathered into our homes!

Is Christmas Over?

Nm 6:22-27
Gal 4:4-7
Lk 2:16-21

Octave of Christmas
Solemnity of Mary, Mother of God

The Church has remembered some very significant people in the days following Christ's birthday: Stephen, the first person to die because he believed in Jesus; John the Apostle, who had the great distinction of being known as "the one Jesus loved" (Jn 20:2a); the Holy Innocents, those little ones who met with the same kind of malice that would eventually kill Jesus; and St. Thomas Becket, whose worldly youth was transformed into heroic defense of the Church when he became a priest. These people and their fates teach us something—something that our society's pattern of celebrating Christmas might have made us forget.

For when we ask ourselves what Christmas means to us today, one week after we celebrated it, many of us can say, "Forgive me, Lord, it doesn't mean much." Perhaps we have found that in our own personal lives we have followed too exactly the pattern the world has developed: Celebrate Christmas Day, and then forget it. Oh, we still light the tree every night and run the trains and go to the post-Christmas sales and try to exchange the gifts that were too much of a surprise for us. From that point of view, Christmas has lingered on. And maybe from that point of view our memory is better than the world's. Because for the world, a Christmas carol a week after Christmas makes little sense.

Lord, Stephen and John and the Holy Innocents and Thomas Becket teach us something we need to know: You ask for consequences in our lives. We cannot celebrate your birth and then ignore you. When you come into the world and into us, you expect us to react. You make a difference, a difference that is sometimes as demanding as death.

Lord, we celebrated your birth. Now help us to remember you in the day-by-day way we live our lives.

Signals of Reality Sir 24:1-4, 8-12
Eph 1:3-6, 15-18
2nd Sunday After Christmas Jn 1:1-18

Many of us have discovered during Christmas the essential simplicity of the mystery we celebrate. It can be said in three words: God became man. But like all concise expressions, the repetition of the words does not guarantee that we understand all their implications.

A man who says to a woman, "I love you," hardly grasps all that he means, and perhaps he never will. The words point to a mystery; and who understands himself completely? Or who can capture all of *love*, no matter what he says? Or who would be so foolish as to think his saying *you* to someone else expresses a total knowledge of that person?

No, words like these refer to simplicities so deep that whole lifetimes are too short to comprehend all their reality. We who are married and who love our spouses know that "I love you" is nothing but a signal of an intense interlocking of realities that must be lived to be appreciated. Our temptation is to substitute words for the realities. But words can bear only so much weight. It is the realities for which we really hunger. We do indeed need the words, but never as replacements for the substance at which they hint.

And so, Lord, when we celebrate the truth that you are God-made-man, we need the reality. We need the sense of who you are, and we need an understanding of what being human really means.

We need, Lord, your love for your Father, your intense interest in him, your intuition that he is love and goodness and kindness and concern. We need your conviction that our world and our lives lose all meaning when we lose God beyond the horizon of our judgment and our desire. And we need, too, some valid sense of our own fragility, our complete dependence, our sin and our sentence of death.

For, Lord, if we go through life thinking we are gods and masters of everything we see, we upset the whole meaning of God-made-flesh. God becomes unimportant; humanity becomes everything. Then we lose touch with the reality of Christmas. Don't let us do that, Lord.

God-With-Us Is 60:1-6
Eph 3:2-3, 5-6
Epiphany Mt 2:1-12

We complete today another Christmas season. Again we have had the chance to think about the Lord's gentle coming into our world as a baby; we have built our customary cribs and lovingly placed in them the statue of the infant Jesus. We have surrounded that figure with the statues of Mary and Joseph and the shepherds and the animals. And today we add the Wise Men, those mysterious figures from the Gentile world used by Matthew to represent all of us whose relationship to Christ is one of faith and not of blood.

These weeks have been a very happy and precious time because they have shown us again that God our Father, when he fulfills a promise, holds nothing back. When Jesus came, he was the living sign that God is never outdone in generosity. He gives us divinity itself.

Ahead of us lies what the Church simply calls the "Ordinary Season of the Year." But our worship during these last few weeks, the love shown, the gifts given, the sharing around our family tables, our reawakened faith in Christ as God-with-us will make these ordinary weeks *extraordinary*. That, after all, is what today, the feast of the Epiphany, is all about. It is the feast which celebrates the manifestation, the "showing-forth," of God among us.

Lord, we celebrate today the homage the heavens pay to you in the form of the star; and we join today in the homage the non-Jewish world pays to you in the Wise Men. You are Lord of heaven and earth. You are God come into our world and our lives; and when you really come, nothing can ever again be the same.

This whole time of Christmas, Lord, when it is lived in faith, casts its warmth into all the days that follow. They will be ordinary; we will not see the decorations in the downtown streets or in our homes. But from another point of view, they will be quite extraordinary. They will be filled with your presence. Lord, you are always God-with-us. Let every day show forth your presence.

A New Creation — Is 42:1-4, 6-7
Acts 10:34-38
Baptism of the Lord — Mt 3:13-17

There is an implication in the Lord's baptism that we need to pray about today, because it is present in our baptisms too. Not only did he identify himself with sinners at his baptism; not only did the Father and the Holy Spirit approve him. His baptism was the sign of something new and powerful beginning in the world. The Father hinted at the newness when he told us to listen to the Son. The Holy Spirit hovered over the Jordan as he hovered over the first chaos, bringing forth a new and ordered world.

Jesus Christ is a new creation, the beginning of a new heaven and a new earth. With his baptism all creation begins anew. As soon as he left the Jordan, the Holy Spirit impelled him to go to the desert, there to pray and to engage and conquer the power of evil. It would not be long before he would begin to preach and choose his apostles, and his work would be made visible to anyone wishing to see. It all began at his baptism.

Lord, the decisive nature of your baptism makes us wonder about ours. You have done everything you could to make our baptisms the beginnings they should be. But, Lord, we wonder whether we have accepted what you did to us when you marked us dead to sin and alive to new life.

And we have reason to wonder. We find in ourselves too much evidence that sin is far from dead; we see lush and vibrant passions, decayed and moldering life. If Baptism has made us open to you as you were open to your Father, we need more concrete signs of that surrender in who we are and what we do.

This confession, Lord, is what can make our celebration of your baptism a healthy goad to our own sluggishness. Help us, at last, at long last, to begin to be what we already are. Help us to learn how to pray and to face the evil in ourselves and in our world. Help us to start saying yes to you.

A Lenten Invitation Jl 2:12-18
 2 Cor 5:20—6:2
Ash Wednesday Mt 6:1-6, 16-18

Lent is a time for generosity. And what an ingrained habit it is for us to be stingy with our love. We look at our married lives, and we see there too many signs of withholding when we should have given openhandedly. We look at our worship and see that we have too often given only the tail-end of our surplus, when what the Lord wanted was our whole selves. So many times we are prodigal in only one way, and that is in pursuing our own advantage.

But the Lord's time is upon us. His grace is urging us to open our eyes to the acceptable moment—today—and to grasp with our heart our real salvation. The misery our selfishness generates is its own proof that we cannot save ourselves; we must look to him. And today is the time to begin.

It is time to turn from a lukewarm half-heartedness and dried-out way of life. It is time to heighten our awareness that God is real and that his touch warms and gives life. The moment has come to turn from the dead-end values that clutter our lives and to learn to appreciate anew the infinite graciousness of a Father whose gifts would stretch our hearts.

Lord Jesus, make us fruitful during this grace-filled time of peace-making. Heal our wounded hearts of the misguided yearnings that weaken their ability to love.

Fill us again with the enthusiasm that made men like Peter and Zaccheus and Francis of Assisi so open to you. Dissolve our cynicism and egoism, our smallness and greed. Help us to prepare ourselves for an Easter in which we will really be able to celebrate the new life you give us.

Lord, you invite us to happiness and peace and a swelling joy. And you invite us *today*. Help us to hear you and to say yes to you today. We do not want to receive God's grace in vain. We want to be alive now and forever.

Temptation in a Good World

Gn 2:7-9; 3:1-7
Rom 5:12-19
Mt 4:1-11

1st Sunday of Lent A

On this first Sunday of Lent it is well for us to reflect on temptation and sin. The Lord himself knew the attractiveness of temptation, but could still say no.

Temptation *is* attractive. Eve was not led into her sin by an offer to become ignorant or dumb or ugly; she was tempted by an invitation to taste the wisdom that belonged to God alone. The Lord was not tempted by offers to eat ashes, or to call the Father powerless, or to brand himself a failure. He was tempted by invitations to take food, to trust that the Father would deliver him from the consequences of a foolish choice, and to seize the lordship of the world he came to win through death. Neither to Eve nor to Christ did sin come dressed in the dusky, bat-winged, cloven-hoofed form artists have created; sin did not offer the ugly and unappealing. Sin offered, in itself, something very good indeed.

And sin has never stopped looking good. Youngsters fall into casual sex because it feels so good. Marriages collapse because another woman or another man is seemingly so much more congenial than a husband or wife. A business executive pays off a government inspector so that the profit sheet can show a larger balance. And so on and on.

Often the object of sin is something that in itself is good. But why then is it sin? For the very simple reason that our choice rejects a higher good. Sex is lovely and good, but only those who are married can make it speak of lasting love. Profits are good, but they are not worth the loss of honesty and justice.

Lord, we ought never to be surprised by temptation in our lives. You were ready for it; Eve was not. What we have to learn is what you taught us: that your Father has a lot to say about how we make this world's goods our own.

Lord, teach us to bless all the goods of this world, but to use only those of which our Father can say: "This is good for *you* here and now."

Light From Within   Gn 12:1-4
2 Tm 1:8-10
2nd Sunday of Lent   A   Mt 17:1-9

Sometimes we awake on a winter's morning and look out on a world transformed during the long night by snow. It puts caps on posts, delicately contoured lips on hills, overhanging blankets on roofs. It blots out all colors and unites them in the one color that contains them all: white. It leaves nothing untouched. And when the storm is finished and before a stunned world begins to stir, there is a deep quiet unlike any other stillness we ever experience. It is a transformation, a transfiguration.

But lovely as it is, it only hints at the transfiguration the Lord experienced in today's Gospel. Snow *covers* things; it is beauty laid on. The difference between this beauty and the Lord's is that his came from within. All the deepest reality that he is shone for a few minutes through his body and even through his clothing. For an instant three men glimpsed eternity. That insistent goodness that we call God transformed the man they called Jesus until the sight intoxicated them with joy.

Lord, you became a prism through whom shone all the beauty of a humanity which had surrendered itself completely to divinity. Yes, Lord, your transfiguration came from within the depth of your being.
And during this Lent you invite us to be transformed into your image. You are not interested in our assuming some kind of overlay of seeming virtue. You want us to be so open to you that your loveliness can become ours where it really counts: in our hearts and our spirits. Lord, transfigure our darkness into your own wonderful light!

The Water of Death and Life   Ex 17:3-7
Rom 5:1-2, 5-8
3rd Sunday of Lent   A   Jn 4:5-42

Most of us experience water in its gentle state, controlled and helpful. We bathe in it, water our lawns with it. We fill our pools with it, irrigate our crops with it. We take it so much for granted—until its wild strength explodes as a hurricane roars up the East coast and high tides sweep away beaches at seaside resorts, or as heavy rains turn tiny creeks into rampaging rivers that inundate whole sections of countryside.

The Lord knew what he was doing when he chose water as the substance that would initiate us into the believing community. He wants us to reflect on some of the qualities of water so that we can understand what happens to us when we are baptized. For Baptism is not some social ritual by which we are given a name; Baptism is a new creation involving all the death and all the life that water can bring.

Water can kill; God made it that way. It can drown and crush and sweep away; it can be terrifying in its savage fury. And all of that quality is present in every Baptism. The early Church could see how death-dealing water can be. In the oldest form of Baptism, the convert went completely into and under the water; to prolong that experience would be to die. In fact, St. Paul saw Baptism exactly as that: a form of death.

Baptized into you, Lord, we are baptized into your death. And your death took you out of the clutches of sin and death. In our Baptism, Lord, we commited ourselves to your life of death to sin.

Lord, water and life and death: how essential, how simple, how close to what your whole mission was all about! As we prepare to celebrate the great baptismal vigil of Holy Saturday night, help us to delve into the meaning of our own Baptism: death to sin and everlasting life in and through you.

In His Light

4th Sunday of Lent   A

1 Sm 16:1, 6-7, 10-13
Eph 5:8-14
Jn 9:1-41

The Lord is the light of the world. He warns us to walk while we have the light, because the night will come when no one can walk or work.

Of course, we have modern conveniences that his world knew nothing about. We can light up our city streets; we can put headlights on our cars; we can keep our factories working 24 hours a day. We seem to have come to the point where we have conquered night and darkness.

But blackouts in places like New York City show us how vulnerable we are when our eyes can no longer see. The city winds down to immobility, and strange and evil forces emerge. Even without blackouts, evil stalks the darker streets and the unprotected parks. We have long since learned that the best protection against crime is a well-lighted house or parking lot.

Lord, you are the light which is the best protection

against all evil. You are the light which enters into the deepest crannies of our hearts to illuminate the darkness of hatred and selfishness. You are the light which envelopes two or more people when they gather to talk and plan and act. You help them see whether what they are about makes ultimate sense or not.

You are the light by which husbands and wives can say: "We need one another; we need our children; everything else is secondary." You are the light which tells a parish that it is a success when its people pray and love. You are the light which guides the young to choose a life and a career of peace-making, justice and kindness over one that wants nothing except self-gain.

Lord, you are our light. Help us never to close our eyes to you. Without you we can only stumble together through the darkness.

The Essential Truth Ez 37:12-14
Rom 8:8-11
5th Sunday of Lent   A Jn 11:1-45

The Gospels for the past two Sundays and for today show Christ in his most basic and essential mission. Two Sundays ago we heard him promise the water of life to the Samaritan woman. Last Sunday he cured the man born blind and called himself the light of the world. Today he brings Lazarus back to life. Conqueror of death, giver of everlasting life, the light by which we live and enjoy life for eternity: all this is what we mean when we call Jesus our redeemer.

Each shows that the Lord is not only God-made-man, but also Emmanuel: God-with-*us*. He came not only to reveal the Father to us but also to draw us into his family and to give us his life, his own Spirit. He is not only God; he is God-*for*-us.

But the sad fact remains, Lord, that we can and do remain unappreciative of your gifts and what they mean for us. You came to destroy death; but you saw death as more than a mere physical cessation of breath. You saw death as a rejection of the one life that endures forever: the life you have with your Father and with the Holy Spirit. Sin is death, and sin is always a prideful lack of love. Why then do we not fear and detest our hatefulness and our malice, our unlawful pleasures, our greed and nasty tongues—all that which separates us from your goodness?

And you are light. Why then, Lord, do we try to solve our most divisive problems in the parish, at home, at work, in the country, or in our own personal lives without prayer to you? We serve you on Sunday and Mammon on Monday. But you said that these things should not be!

Lord, in these last weeks of Lent drive deeply into our hearts the most essential of all your truths: We need you every day so that we can live rightly, die as Christians and rejoice eternally. You are God-with-us every instant; help us to be with you every instant.

Why, Lord?	Is 50:4-7
	Phil 2:6-11
Passion Sunday (Palm Sunday) A	Mt 26:14–27:66

Sometimes we wonder why the Lord found it necessary to go through all the suffering we remember this week. He said goodbye to all those whom he loved so much, which is the most piercing kind of pain any one experiences. He wept a bloody prayer at Gethsemane which simply tells us that his will and the Father's had to be welded together in a fire of torment. He endured the thorns and the nails and the cross, the signs of the malice of those to whom he offered love—and spurned love is another peculiarly human agony.

Why was all this necessary? Why couldn't the Lord have merely issued a divine decree that all of us were saved and were now members of his family? Why was suffering the road he took to bring us life? Only the Lord himself knows the final answer. But perhaps that answer is rooted in his knowledge that nothing less could move us.

That, Lord, would be horrifying. That would imply that we would never have learned what you really had done except by seeing you on a cross. It would mean that we were so blind to ourselves and to the miserable ways we were using our freedom that a body on a cross was the only way to heal blindness. It would suggest that we had so distorted our precious power to love that only the most powerful of shock treatments could restore us. In a word, Lord, it says that we and our sin put you on the cross.

Lord, sin must be so ugly. Malice and hate, cruelty and injustice poison a world that was created good throughout. Sin attacks that goodness and the Father who created it. You set yourself in opposition to the evil with which we are destroying ourselves and your world. And what a price you paid. Lord Jesus, let each of us think about Gethsemane and Calvary this week. Maybe we will finally stop being so stupid and destructive and suicidal. But we need your help. When has it ever been otherwise?

Sin and Death Defeated

Easter Sunday

Acts 10:34, 37-43
Col 3:1-4 or 1 Cor 5:6-8
Jn 20:1-9

He did it! He entered into a fight with two of the most terrifying opponents any of us will ever meet: sin and death. And he won.

But how important it is to bring those two abstract concepts—sin and death—down to our own personal level. Sin is terrifying because it is so brutal and pitiless, so cold and inhuman. Sin is what is in the heart of a man who waits in the dark for an unsuspecting woman to pass and then attacks and mutilates her. Sin can sit around a corporation board table and decide on the necessity of war so that sales can increase. Sin can hold a gun and mercilessly put a bullet in a hostage's head.

Sin has no heart. It may have intelligence, and it may be strong; but it does not know the meaning of love. Sin pins the Lord to a cross and laughs at him there. He knew sin better than we know it; he suffered from it. And he knows death better than we know it. All of us still stand on this side of that dread door. He went through it, and in no gentle way, either.

What horrifying realities sin and death are! And what a gain to the world and to us to have someone say to them: "This far and no further. You have hurt my creation and my people too long. Back to the depths from which you came."

Lord, you want no more sin in this lovely and good world you have made. You want a world where people may walk in peace, unafraid of one another and conscious of each other's needs, a world where we are as ingenious in love as those who do not hear you are adept in hate. Lord Jesus, you want us to be dead to sin and to live in this world as if we were already in heaven. Why else did you die except to remove the reality of sin from our lives? And why else did you rise except to bring us already the joy and peace of heaven?

Lord, we thank you and praise you, and we cry out with all creation today: "Alleluia! He is risen!"

Struggling to Believe　　　　　　Acts 2:42-47
　　　　　　　　　　　　　　　　　　1 Pt 1:3-9
2nd Sunday of Easter　A　　　　　Jn 20:19-31

Certain people in Scripture are appealing because they are so human: Peter weeping, Zaccheus perched in the limbs of a tree, the woman trembling in the crowd after her flow of blood had stopped. And Thomas.

Thomas is no stranger to most of us. We understand his reaction. If any of us were told that three days after Hubert Humphrey had died he was seen walking in the corridors of the Capitol, we would have our difficulties, even if 10 of our best friends told us they had seen him. Thomas and we are made of the same cloth, but then so are we and Judas and Peter and Zaccheus and the woman. They were human, and so are we.

Jesus understood them all and continues to understand us. He did not disown Peter; he was kind to Zaccheus and the woman. He tried desperately to bring Judas back. And as for Thomas—he did just what was right for the doubting disciple. He came to him, spoke with him, invited him to touch—and Thomas responded with a more perfect act of faith than any of the others had made. And we don't even know if he actually did touch the Lord!

Thomas came to his faith by a difficult route. Some of us are travelling that same path. Others are saying: "I cannot believe; I do not believe enough; Jesus to me is a word, but little else. I don't know him, and I can't see what he means to me." And maybe others of us profess belief, but only with our lips, and in our hearts doubt as much as Thomas ever did.

No matter, Lord. You know us, and you know how human we are. You knew the perfect way to handle Thomas, and you know the perfect way to handle us. All we can say, Lord, is make us like the Thomas who professed you as Lord and God, rather than the Thomas who said, "I will never believe. . . ." (Jn 20: 25b). His faith in you is a sign of what can happen to us, too.

Lord Jesus, none of us have ever seen you. Increase our faith so we can hear you say of us:
  Blest are they who have not seen
    and have believed (Jn 20:29b).

Catch Up with Us

Acts 2:14, 22-28
1 Pt 1:17-21
Lk 24:13-35

3rd Sunday of Easter   A

How strange and yet how ordinary those days after the Lord's death were to those who loved him! After his cruel crucifixion, they crept into hiding. A few had the courage to claim his body and to bury him in haste, but what a dreary Sabbath it must have been. If it were really a day of rest for them, it must have been a despairing and sad rest.

But that first day of the week! Will we ever understand its impact? First those courageous and loving women and then Peter and John find the tomb empty. Mary Magdalene hears him call her name. And the women see angels.

Today we hear again the story of the two disciples leaving Jerusalem to go to Emmaus. What was in their hearts? Emptiness? Bewilderment? Doubt? They had heard the women's news, and still they left the city. Again the Lord pursued them just as he pursued Thomas in his doubt and—thanks and praise—just as he always pursues us until he has us.

The Lord's conversation with these two must have been a searing yet loving experience for them. They were still so naive in their understanding; even after Christ's death they were still thinking of him as the political leader who might have restored independence to their beloved country. Jesus had to correct that expectation, and although he began with a rebuke he must have continued with a gentleness and a love that completely captured them, because they simply would not let him leave. And he stayed with them until they did recognize him in the breaking of the bread.

Lord Jesus, you made your disciples' hearts burn and yearn as you talked with them. You allowed them to know you as you broke bread. Make us burn, too, with love for you as we hear you in the Scriptures. Open our eyes to see you in the bread broken for us at each

Eucharist. Walk with us, Lord, and let us be witnesses to you in your risen and glorious life.

When we start to walk away from Jerusalem, catch up with us, strengthen us and make us turn back. Lord, make us *real* members of your believing Church!

We Hear Your Voice Acts 2:14, 36-41
  1 Pt 2:20-25
4th Sunday of Easter   A Jn 10:1-10

We need never have any doubt that the Lord knows us. He knows us inside out. He knows when we rise and when we sit. He has counted every hair on our heads. He knows where we aim in whatever we do, even when we miss so badly that we hurt ourselves and others.

Because he knows us so well—and because he lived, suffered and rejoiced, was tempted and died like us—we can be thankful that he is our judge. For if ever a judge will lean towards mercy and understanding, he will. If the price he paid to win us was death, he certainly will sympathize with us; we cannot doubt that he wants us. Despite all our sin, he sees something in us that outweighs even Calvary. He is the shepherd who was killed defending his sheep.

And we are the sheep. But are we *his* sheep? Do we recognize his voice when he says to us: "How blest are the poor in spirit" (Mt 5:3a)? Or do we find another voice more inviting which says: "Blessed is the one who can say: 'I got mine' "?

He says: "If. . .your brother has anything against you, leave your gift at the altar, go first to be reconciled with your brother, and then come and offer your gift" (Mt 5:23b-24). Another voice might say: "Get even; don't let anybody put anything over on you." Which voice makes sense to us?

Lord, the things you say are sometimes very hard to grasp and to do, and we do not always find ourselves

willing to listen. And so we stray, sure that what we want is better than what you want. But after we stray we soon find ourselves in desert places. We are lost until we hear again your Good Shepherd's voice: "My yoke is easy and my burden light" (Mt 11:30). Lord, we can be so foolish; keep us close to you, we beg you.

You Fill Our Hunger Acts 6:1-7
1 Pt 2:4-9
5th Sunday of Easter   A Jn 14:1-12

    The Lord's words in today's Gospel speak to a great and yearning hunger in the heart of each of us. We are everlastingly restless and unquiet, always wanting more than we have, always with eyes fixed on the future, anxious to be anywhere but here. Perhaps it was with this unsatisfied hunger that the serpent tempted Eve: "You will be like gods" (Gn 3:5a). Certainly it was that hunger that made the great and worldly-wise St. Augustine say: "Our hearts are restless until they rest in you."

    We have an eternal quest eating at our hearts. Our whole being is like a piece of metal straining towards a magnet out of sight and out of reach. It is not so much that we want God; it is more that we *need* him and are completely at loose ends until we find him.

    Perhaps the whole story of our foolish sins is a tale of missing the mark, shortsighted attempts to seize the Father in all the good he has built into our world. We grasp, but we so often miss. We want so much to see him, but too often we stop short of him.

    And then, Lord, we hear you say: "Whoever has seen me has seen the Father" (Jn 14:9b). No wonder you can also say your yoke is easy, your burden light. For when you satisfy our deepest longing, Lord, we are indeed finally at peace. When we can see God now in all of your truth and loveliness, we already have begun our heaven. And all we need do to see God is to see you,

Lord. You show him to us as clearly as we will ever see him before we die.

So, Lord, we see you curing the sick, forgiving the sinner, raising the dead, befriending people from every walk of life, caressing children, confronting hypocrites, giving yourself in so many ways. And we say: "This is God." And we are happy, Lord. You have shown us a Father. Never let us turn him into anything less.

Never Alone

Acts 8:5-8, 14-17
1 Pt 3:15-18

6th Sunday of Easter   A

Jn 14:15-21

In so many ways the Lord identifies with us. He calls us the branches of his vine; he gives us his own body. He tells us that his life is ours and his conquest of death our victory. In today's Gospel he gives us still another sign of how close he is to us. He promises to return to us, never to leave us, even after his death:

I will not leave you orphaned;
I will come back to you (Jn 14:18).

But we sometimes ask ourselves, especially when we are discouraged or weak or very lonely: "Is Jesus really that close to me?" In moments like these we must remember his promise to send the Spirit, who will be with us always. He meant what he said. This new Advocate will not come and go according to our moods. He will be with us *always*, every day, every minute. His whole role is to make us members of God's family. We ought never again to consider ourselves orphans, as if our Father had died.

Lord, when we forget, then we fail. But our forgetfulness is so foolish. It's not as if you were giving us a hard intellectual riddle to unravel and to remember. What you are really saying to us is:

... you can recognize him
because he remains with you

and will be within you (Jn 14:17b).
You ask us to remember that we are alive, not dead; that our life is yours, not ours alone; that you are always with us in your Spirit, and that we never are by ourselves.

Why is that so hard to accept, Lord? And yet so often we do not accept it, and we do forget. Perhaps we need St. Peter to remind each one of us, "Venerate the Lord. . .in your hearts" (1 Pt 3:15a). And maybe we need too to hear him say: "Keep your conscience clear" (1 Pt 3:16a).

Lord, keep us from sin. Keep close to us. And let us know the joy of your nearness!

Invitation to Christian Maturity   Acts 1:1-11
                                        Eph 1:17-23
Ascension   A   Mt 28:16-20

Sometimes we wonder which feast of the Church year most accurately reflects the kind of life we really are living. It certainly is not Christmas. "Christmas spirit" so identifies only a particular time that we are surprised to see it show up outside December. It seems not to be Easter either, because—even though we are ashamed to say it—the Lord's resurrection is not always in the front of our minds. Nor do we seem to be living in that exuberance of the Spirit that Pentecost brought to the first believers.

Perhaps the feast that best characterizes the lives of most of us is the Ascension. This feast commemorates Christ's leaving our sight to be once again at his Father's side. It invites us to take our Christian maturity to the point where it can say: "The Lord has left; now I am to become a Christian."

Lord, that stance may be precisely where most of us always seem to be: aware that you are absent from us physically, aware that you want something from us, aware that we have a calling to fulfill—yet not doing very much and certainly not being Christians with the fullness with which you were the Christ.

We look at our jobs, and while we may do them as professionals we do not always do them as Christians. We live in our homes, but not always as Christian mothers and fathers and children. We fulfill our Sunday obligation of worship, but we do not really celebrate joyously our Christianity.

Lord Jesus, you do not want us to be perpetually waiting. You do not want us only to be Christians of the Ascension, "looking up at the skies" (Acts 1:11a). You want us to be aware that the gift of God has already been given to us. The Spirit is already ours. We are Pentecost Christians. Lord, shake us from our blindness and wake us to your light!

Waiting in Prayer Acts 1:12-14
1 Pt 4:13-16
7th Sunday of Easter   A Jn 17:1-11

There is something incomplete about a Christian who is always waiting for that final push before doing almost anything for the Lord and his kingdom. Yet many of us are perpetually in the wings waiting for our Christian cue—and maybe shaking with fright that it might come. Today we pray again the prayer of those frightened believers who cowered together in that upstairs room waiting for something to happen.

They believed in Jesus Christ. So do we. They were fascinated by him. So are we. They knew his life, his death and his resurrection. So do we. They had received his message. So have we. But they had done almost nothing yet to spread it. And neither have we.

Perhaps what the Lord's followers did during those days from the Ascension to the coming of the Holy Spirit is a challenge and an invitation to all of us who have come after them and who know the pleasantness and the safety of inactivity! "Together they devoted themselves to constant prayer" (Acts 1:14a). They did not preach or work miracles or make converts during those days; all they did was pray.

Lord, you know that we are not exactly miracle workers either. You also know how few of us are constant in prayer. And you wait for us to be constant in prayer *together*.

Lord, help us reflect on our worship. Do we pray together and deeply? We think of this last week. How strong a part did prayer play during it? We see our world; we know how much it needs you. How much are we praying to prepare it and ourselves for you? Lord Jesus, not all of us will be like Peter and Paul in miraculous works; but each of us can be a disciple in constant prayer. And then when the Spirit does come, anything can happen!

Our Hearts Are Empty Vessels   Acts 2:1-11
                                    1 Cor 12:3-7, 12-13
Pentecost Sunday   Jn 20:19-23

Before his death, the Lord told his friends it was best for them that he should leave them, so that the Holy Spirit could come to them. Those words must have puzzled the apostles. They knew what they had in Jesus, and they must have thought nothing could be better. He was all they wanted or needed. But the Lord wanted something more for them. And when the Spirit did come, they understood. How desperately they needed him! How desperately *we* need him!

Like the apostles, we can be very fearful. We can hesitate to mention Christ's name, even to our wife or husband or children, let alone to those at work. We can be sad so often, weak so much, lazy and without enthusiasm and devotion so easily. Our hearts can be cold to the poor who hold out their hands to us. But our passions can burn when we rush after our own pleasure. And we can be so wounded by sin and empty of the Lord's presence. We can be just plain miserable when he seems to have disappeared from our sight and our values.

Lord, you know us well. You said you know what is in our hearts. You see our guilt and our wounds and all our cowardice and laziness. But you promised not to leave us orphaned. Dear Lord, how we need that promise, and how we today, this minute, need the way you fulfilled that promise for your first followers. When your Spirit rushed on them, they forgot themselves and their own petty problems and began lives so unselfish that not even cruel martyrdom could make them cry "Enough!"

Lord Jesus, send your Spirit on us today. Refresh us. Cool our passions. Heal our wounds. Make us strong. Cleanse our consciences. Give us a sense of your constant presence. Lord, give us the joy of your salvation!

A Foolish Question

Ex 34:4-6, 8-9
2 Cor 13:11-13
Jn 3:16-18

Sunday After Pentecost
Trinity Sunday   A

Sometimes we look at our Catholic lives, and we have to shake our heads just a little bit. We seem to be hung up on obligations: We must get to Mass on Sunday or risk mortal sin. We must receive Holy Communion at Easter time or break a serious Church law. We must not eat meat on Fridays during Lent. We must do this and we must not do that. When we go to confession, we find ourselves ticking off all the times we have failed in all those obligations, big and small. And many of us wonder, "Is this all there is to being a Catholic?"

No, it surely is not! The Lord did not die to force us to come to a Mass that bores us or to grumble over an egg sandwich on a Lenten Friday. Calvary was fought for bigger stakes than a listless hour in Church or an unsatisfied palate. He died as he lived: to show everyone that the Father is real, and he was faithful to him because he loved him. Even death could not make the Lord cease saying and doing what he was sent to say and do. He died so that he could give everyone the vital gift of the Spirit. That is the answer to our foolish question: "Is this all there is to being a Catholic?"

Lord, we ask that question only when we still do not really know you as our brother, our life, our shepherd, our head. That question is possible only when God is *not* our Father; when we have not yet allowed him to enter our closest family circle. And that question arises only when *our* spirit has not been personally open to the *Holy* Spirit. In other words, Lord, when the Holy Trinity is only a comfortable doctrine that we can say yes to with our lips, and not yet a fiercely loving family of three persons pulling us into the vortex of their happiness and their self-gift to each other, then our Catholicism is an easy religion of do's and don'ts.

Lord, on this feast of the Holy Trinity, make us into Catholics whose whole happiness is to know, love and serve the Father, you and the Spirit.

Food That Gives Life　　　　　　　Dt 8:2-3, 14-16
　　　　　　　　　　　　　　　　　　1 Cor 10:16-17
Corpus Christi　A　　　　　　　　　Jn 6:51-58

In today's Gospel the Lord is absolutely clear about why he wants us to receive Holy Communion: He wants us to live. Of course, he was speaking to a crowd of skeptics who knew that they already were alive. And his promise offered no guarantee against the physical process of dying; he only promised to raise up on the last day those who ate his body and drank his blood. The life of which he spoke is not the life we have because blood flows through our veins. It's another kind of life, independent of the life we received from our parents and yet in some way intimately involved with it.

The life Jesus wants to give us has a beginning in us, but it need never have an end. The Lord in his humanity is its channel and in his divinity is its source. The life he gives is a joining in the life of the Godhead from which he came. It is a life which can allow us to say, without any trace of falsehood: "I am a child of God." It is a life which begins at Baptism and is nourished every time we approach the altar to receive him. It is a life we live every time we act the way Christ acted and love the way he loved. It is the life he had in mind when he urged us to become perfect like the Father, for the Father is love.

This kind of life, Lord, does not bow to death. Death came into this world because of sin. But you, Lord, conquered sin and death by your love on Golgotha. You freed us from sin to pass through the gate of our physical death into the full flowering of the eternal life you planted in us when you welcomed us at Baptism.

Lord Jesus, the life you strengthen in us at each Communion is the constant love and reality of the Holy Trinity, and it is a vital and urgent process that will never allow us to be satisfied with sin or apathy. We who have been fed at your table love you and bless you. Help us to live in your love!

The Radiance of God Is 49:3, 5-6
1 Cor 1:1-3
2nd Sunday   A Jn 1:29-34

Many of us have fireplaces in our homes. We know what it is to see that black and yawning hole when no fire is in it. We know too what it is to take the fire screen away, to arrange kindling and logs and start a flame. Sometimes the fire catches at once; sometimes the logs are stubborn, and we have to start over again. But when the fire is really leaping and popping, we know the joy of sitting before it with our children around us. The black, gaping hole has now become a mass of pulsing flame, beautiful to see and comforting to feel.

But not only our houses contain black and yawning holes that should be filled with light and warmth. We find emptiness and darkness in our lives, too. We see ourselves pursuing pleasures that excite us for a minute and then leave us void. We know too many days spent in a silly race for tinsel—a little more money, our picture in the paper, a pat on the back from the boss. We know, too, the bitter pleasures of getting even with somebody, even of hurting people we love. Our days are not always radiant with the light of the Lord shining through us. We can extinguish it with vanity and malice, apathy and weakness.

That, Lord, is why we need you so much. You are the one of whom Isaiah speaks, the light sent to all the nations. Where once there was the darkness of sin, you bring the light of love. Where once there was the blindness of ignorance, you bring the clarity of truth. Where once there was the cold of bigotry and distance, you bring the warmth of companionship around you and your table.

Lord, you take the sin of the world away. Nobody else could do that—no guru, no psychiatrist, no doctor, or lawyer or even priest—even he works always in your name. Darkness, cold, enmity, hatred—these are not our best climates, Lord. We do not grow well in them, but become pale and withered. We need you, you who are light and life and love. Lord, light our world with the fire of your love and let us know the joy of being gathered around you forever.

A Light in the Darkness

3rd Sunday A

Is 8:23–9:3
1 Cor 1:10-13, 17
Mt 4:12-23

All of us have experienced a power failure. All of a sudden the lights go out, the TV fades and we sit stunned in a darkness that is not of our making and that we do not like. As we stumble around smashing into furniture and upsetting vases, we give ourselves a practical lesson in the wisdom of the old adage: "Better to light one candle than to curse the darkness."

The world was like that darkened living room before the Lord came: stumbling people looking for some kind of meaning, hurting themselves and one another, seeing little or no light, uncomprehending in the midst of a disorder they had inherited and then helped to perpetuate. But who can blame them? Not the Lord. He had pity on them; he called them "sheep without a shepherd" (Mk 6:34b). To them only a little light had been given; and so he expected only a small return.

But from us, Lord, you expect a greater return. Because when you came you brought light for all to see and you expect us to open our eyes.

Sometimes we play games with you—the way we used to play as children. We shut our eyes and pretend that everything has vanished because we can't see it anymore. But nothing has vanished, Lord; the world is still there. The poor we were so concerned about at Christmas are still looking for food a month later. The committees we were going to join at church or in town are still looking for our help. The talk we were going to have with our troubled son or daughter is still needed. Fetuses are still being aborted; children are still in need of foster homes; hospitals are still asking for volunteers.

You told us the poor would always be with us. Closing our eyes to them does not make them go away. You also warned us to cherish your presence; yet we close our eyes to our need for you and do not pray. Lord, open our eyes. Give us your light.

A Noble Ancestry

4th Sunday A

Zep 2:3; 3:12-13
1 Cor 1:26-31
Mt 5:1-12

If we were to raise our eyes to look at the people around us in church on Sunday, we might be surprised to see how closely that group resembles the people St. Paul speaks about today. We are not the powerful ones of this world. We are housewives and stenographers; office-managers and government workers; gas-station workers and machinists; bakers, teachers, lawyers and doctors. Most of us do not have to search far through our ancestry to find people whose fingernails were always dirty and whose world was limited to a farmhouse and a small patch of land. We are not the wellborn or the aristocrats.

But maybe our ancestry is really elite. Our ancestors were the people oldest in the faith: the city-workers St. Paul speaks of and the fishermen the Lord invited to be with him. Our ancestry is not in a bloodline; it is in the brotherhood and sisterhood of those whom the Lord called his brothers and sisters: "whoever does the will of my heavenly Father" (Mt 12:50b).

So we start wellborn. But that is no reason for us ever to glory in our ancestry. Jesus had little sympathy with the Pharisees when they claimed special treatment because Abraham was their father. No, what he wanted was not some kind of family pride based on an illustrious ancestor. What he wanted—and still wants—was a mindset in each of us like the spirit of Abraham who always was ready to obey; or Zaccheus who really got excited when Jesus came; or Peter, James and John who left everything to follow him.

Their glory is theirs, and we must not claim it. Our glory must be in imitating those first ancestors of ours who followed Christ with a love that sometimes led them to death.

Lord Jesus, help us to be poor in spirit, thirsty for holiness, merciful and single-hearted. These are the fam-

ily characteristics of all of your brothers and sisters in every generation. We know that we still have much to learn; but others have learned, and so can we. But no one ever learned without you, and neither will we. Help us really to be your followers!

Letting Our Light Shine   Is 58:7-10
1 Cor 2:1-5
5th Sunday   A   Mt 5:13-16

How simple today's readings are! They all say some of the most important things we have to hear if we want to call ourselves Christians. Paul assures his beloved Corinthians that Jesus is absolutely essential. He is their life; he saved them from death; he loved them and made them his brothers and sisters. Everything else that Paul writes is based on that. Even when his writings are most complicated and difficult he still is trying to say the simplest thing: Without the Lord, we are nothing.

The Gospel speaks as simply. Paul says that the Lord is everything to us and Jesus says that we are to be everything to the people around us. If we are really Christian!" We are simply to be so radiant that starving eyes and hearts turn to us for light.

And we are radiant not because we have turned on our own lighting system, but because God's love shines through us. We will be judged on ordinary kindnesses like giving a drink to someone who is thirsty, or food to someone who is hungry, or clothing to someone who is naked.

Lord, Isaiah knew you only as a mysterious figure yet to come. But he anticipated your teaching when he spoke of:
Sharing your bread with the hungry,
  sheltering the oppressed and the homeless;
Clothing the naked when you see them,
  and not turning your back on your own.

Then your light will break forth like the dawn. . .
(Is 58:7-8a)

It's not very complicated, Lord; forgive us when we twist your message of light to our own dark purposes. Light to you is simple goodness. And what is so hard about that?

Time for Housecleaning

6th Sunday   A

Sir 15:15-20
1 Cor 2:6-10
Mt 5:17-37

All of us have been amused by little scenes on TV in which a husband, left alone for a few days of housekeeping, sweeps a pile of dirt under a rug or stuffs a pair of dirty socks behind the bed. He would like things to be clean and orderly, but he is not quite sure of what to do or energetic enough to do it.

And there we have a picture of ourselves. We would like to clear our lives of all the mess that clutters them. We would like to be open and clear in the Lord's sight. But sometimes, maybe most times, we don't know how to do it; or, knowing, we don't have the energy. So we shift the dust on the surface, or we stuff things out of sight. But in important matters like our relationship with Christ, nothing will stay hidden for long. Open the door and out everything tumbles.

Perhaps we are faced with a nagging problem like pilfering from the company where we work. We assure ourselves that a big company will never notice the missing wrench. And so we hem and haw; we steal and are troubled. We push the real solution out of sight and sweep the situation under the rug—maybe with the brush we stole.

Or we know that the fascinating conversations we are having with the girl at the next desk are getting *too* fascinating; and we know where we are heading. We also know the solution, but we keep heading it off so that it won't make any demands on our pleasure.

Lord Jesus, you tell us today that sin starts in our head and in our heart. You tell us that a final caving in to a sinful act has been preceded by the erosion of our will. You tell us to clear our head of bad ideas and our heart of bad desires. You make sense, Lord. Why do we wait until we are overwhelmed? That makes *no* sense!

Meeting Gospel Standards   Lv 19:1-2, 17-18
1 Cor 3:16-23
7th Sunday   A   Mt 5:38-48

Something is so much taken for granted in today's readings that unless we isolate it and appreciate it we could be discouraged by what we hear. For we do not find it easy to turn the other cheek when somebody has just slapped us. Being hit is so humiliating that we never forget persons who have demeaned us this way. Nor can we lightly relinquish our just claims to what is ours when somebody else wants it. We know how we feel when a neighbor tries to put a fence up three feet into our yard. The kind of things asked of us in today's Gospel is hard.

But some people have heeded. Thomas More saw his holdings go and still did not hate his king. Mother Teresa of Calcutta goes through life wanting very little for herself but begging shamelessly for the poor untouchables she finds in the streets of India. And a lot of fathers and mothers never taste white meat from a turkey or chicken once the kids start to like it. Our world is laced with more saintliness than we sometimes think. The question is why saintliness should be appealing in spite of its difficulty.

But the answer to that question, Lord, is involved with what is taken for granted in today's readings—our conviction that God our Father is someone so great and someone we love so much that we want to be like him. For, Lord, you offer no other motive to us to do the things that you ask except that they will prove that we are his sons and daughters. Turning the other cheek, giving up just claims and being generous beyond the wildest expectations of those who make demands are characteristics of your Father. All you're saying, Lord, is that they should be ours, too.

But what, Lord, if we don't see your Father as that kind and generous? Suppose we see him as a hardhearted judge and taskmaster? Well, Lord, that is our loss, and our life will reflect it. You see your Father as the most loving and lovable reality there is. Share your vision with us.

With a Parent's Love

8th Sunday   A

Is 49:14-15
1 Cor 4:1-5
Mt 6:24-34

The prophet Isaiah is very comforting today as he tells us that God remembers us even more intimately than a mother remembers the child formed from her own flesh. And those of us who are mothers—or fathers—know how much our child is part of our love and our hopes, our joys and our sufferings. We have experienced how much our lives are affected by the little one who appears in our household, and how our hearts are warmed when a baby's fingers curl around ours for the first time.

Our children are part of ourselves; the Father made us that way. He wants us to experience in our limited way what he experiences in his infinite way when he sees each one of us. We cannot forget our child. And the Father can never forget us.

The Lord is even more explicit than Isaiah in saying the same thing. He says that our Father knows us down to our last intimate detail, even to how many strands of hair we have on our head. That is staggering. It means that we live our life immersed in a love that stops at no boundaries. It means that graciousness enfolds us in an infinite tenderness that never abandons us even when we abandon it and even when we do not know its presence.

Lord Jesus, we can and do forget your Father's love for us. And when that happens our crosses become meaningless, our sorrow and weariness and fear have no remedy. Our horizon constricts around us until we think that we are alone in a world whose purpose is our merciless destruction. But, Lord, that is exactly the vision from which you came to deliver us. We are not alone. We are children swaddled in an infinite love. Lord, fill our hearts with the joy of your nearness!

Building Solid Foundations Dt 11:18, 26-28
Rom 3:21-25, 28
9th Sunday   A Mt 7:21-27

Many of us like to lie in our beds listening to the patter of rain as it strikes the roof above us or the window that protects us from the wet chill. We are thankful for the soundness of our house, and we dig deeply into our blankets until we fall asleep. That kind of storm does not bother us; we are sheltered.

But in less-protected places, the rain and the wind become driving enemies, and we wish for nothing else except to escape their strength. A few of us have known the horror of a flood. We have seen foul and muddy water tearing away the doors and windows of our house and have felt the whole house lurch and begin to disintegrate under the insane battering of the stampeding waters.

Today's Gospel echoes that last kind of experience. The Lord tells us it is not only water that can sweep our peaceful security away. All sorts of trials, all sorts of confusions and troubles can attack our lives. And we can lose ourselves unless we have something solid to build on and to cling to. A tottering marriage will fail without help; a youngster drawn to drugs will be wrecked if he is left to his own strength; a bitter and revengeful person will hurt his enemy if nothing stops him.

Lord, we seem so easily to grasp the apple of our destruction. We think we will be satisfied if we solve our own problems by our own means, and we forget so quickly the times we have tried our own solutions in the past and have been swept away by our passions, our greed, our foolishness.
Your word is very clear. We invite personal disaster when we forget that you alone are the foundation on which we must build our lives. We never taught ourselves to love God with all our strength and our neighbor as ourselves. You taught us that, Lord, and there alone is our peace. Our other solutions are always faulty. Lord, give us the grace to hear and heed you and so learn where happiness truly lies.

True Worship

10th Sunday   A

Hos 6:3-6
Rom 4:18-25
Mt 9:9-13

The first and third readings of today's Mass stress something that we who call ourselves "good Catholics" must always remember; because when we do, we will really be "good." Through Hosea, God says that he wants love and not sacrifice. Jesus says almost the same thing in the Gospel. Hosea was speaking to the people of Judah and Ephraim, and Jesus was speaking to the Pharisees. But both were also speaking to us.
What Jesus says to us is very simple: God is not satisfied with a religious worship that looks only towards him and that never thinks of the human beings with whom we live. God would rather not have us call him "Father" if we have not yet learned how to say "brother" and "sister."

God does not want sacrifices if people offer them with pride and hate in their hearts. God does not want us offering bread and wine if our hands are closed to those around us. God does not hear us crying, "Lord, Lord," when our own ears are closed to the pleas of those who beg our help.

Lord, you repeat all this so often. You tell us to leave our offering at the altar and seek reconciliation with one another before offering our gift. You tell us to ask our Father to forgive us to the extent that we forgive others—a frightening prayer for those of us who say once in a while: "I can never forgive that person for what she did to me." Your apostle John tells us that we are liars when we claim to love a God whom we can't see while all the time hating a brother whom we can.

Lord, help us to be right on this point. Help us towards a real mercy and a real love that includes our brothers and our sisters. For without that mercy and love, our sacrifices to God can destroy us. But with them our worship rises like incense to a Father whose love excludes no one, no one at all.

Imitating the Father　　　　　　　　Ex 19:2-6
　　　　　　　　　　　　　　　　　　　Rom 5:6-11
11th Sunday　A　　　　　　　　　　　Mt 9:36–10:8

Several times the Lord says how important it is for us to do towards others what he and the Father have first done towards us. He tells us to imitate the perfection of the Father. He relates the story of the servant whose employer forgives him a huge debt but who learns nothing from that mercy. As Paul says, Jesus died for us while we were still sinners. The Lord completes the circle when he teaches us to pray: "Forgive us as we forgive."

In today's Gospel St. Matthew says: "At the sight of the crowds [Jesus'] heart was moved with pity. They were lying prostrate from exhaustion, like sheep without a shepherd" (Mt 9:36). He provided them with shepherds; he called the apostles and sent them out to do what he had been doing. And his parting words commanded them to give the gift they had received.

Lord, John the Evangelist must have had all this in mind when he wrote: "God is love" (1 Jn 4:16b). Indeed he is. And the Father invites everyone who shares his life to imitate him. You came forth from the Father in love; you sent the apostles so that your love could be known by as many people as possible. You who gave so much wanted your friends to know the joy of giving. Lord, your Father and you are the greatest gift-givers ever, and you want that same generosity of heart to be ours too.

Do not allow us, Lord, to be so possessive of our Catholicism that we feel no urge to share it. Do not let us sit on our hands while yours are outstretched on a cross. Do not permit us to think that our Father will be satisfied if we say "Thanks" to him but "No thanks" to our brothers and sisters.

Lord, your Father began a circle of love when he sent you. He needs us to complete that circle with one another, and he wants *all* of our voices saying, "*Our Father.*" Lord, lose none of us whom the Father gave you!

Proclaiming God's Wonders　　　　Jer 20:10-13
　　　　　　　　　　　　　　　　　　Rom 5:12-15
12th Sunday　A　　　　　　　　　Mt 10:26-33

The Lord tells us in today's Gospel not to be afraid to proclaim him from the housetops, to acknowledge him on earth if we expect to be acknowledged before the Father in heaven. How, then, can our tongues be so strangely silent? Not only are we not on our housetops; too many of us are not even saying "Lord" in our hearts. And maybe that is precisely why our tongues are tied. Maybe we spend too little time reviewing to ourselves all the signs of the Father's care. Jesus tells us today that not even a little sparrow is ever out of the Father's loving sight—and certainly neither are we.

Lord, sometimes we must strike ourselves on the breast and say: "I have been a weak Catholic. I have not made your name known to others, and I have been ashamed of your gospel. I have forgotten you in my joys and in the sorrows of others. Sometimes, Lord, the only time I am awake to your reality is when sickness, disaster or death threaten my own happiness."

Lord, help us to believe in the care your Father has for us. Help us to see his hand at work in the family he has given us, in the good jobs we have, in the love we see in others' eyes. For he is infallibly at work. And when faith allows us to see him, Lord, help us acknowledge his goodness and kindness to us, first in prayer and then to our family and those around us. Untie our tongues so that we might proclaim how wonderful you and your Father are!

Words That Make Us Squirm 2 Kgs 4:8-11, 14-16
Rom 6:3-4, 8-11
13th Sunday   A Mt 10:37-42

Sometimes the Lord's words can make us very uncomfortable. It's not the type of discomfort we feel when we hear somebody tell an outright lie or mention something that is grotesquely out of place. No, he is rather like a skilled doctor who probes and asks, "Does it hurt here?" We say, "You bet it does."

The kind of discomfort the Lord causes is the unease we feel when his words confront our fumbling lives and we must admit: "Lord, you're hurting me. I am not what you want me to be." It's a good hurt; we need it if we are ever to make sense of our lives.

One sentence in today's Gospel can make many of us squirm: "He who seeks only himself brings himself to ruin" (Mt 10:39a). We see in our lives a lot of self-seeking: the priest whose work is only what he wants to do, whose ears are closed to needs he alone could meet if his heart were loving enough to care; the parents whose social lives would be "so much nicer if it only weren't for the children." There are husbands who either cannot or will not understand that women might possibly think and feel differently from men, and wives who will not understand what a husband's workday might do to his patience. There are young people who see life only as a kind of massive ego-trip; and children whose toys may be touched by absolutely no one but themselves.

Lord, all of us who have drifted into stances like these know there is no happiness in them. We know we are miserable and we can sense how unhappy those around us are. Selfishness, Lord, is hardly a fertile ground for bliss. But we find the lesson so hard to learn.

That's why, Lord, we need your painful words: "He who seeks only himself brings himself to ruin." And why we need the cure you offer to us: "He who brings himself to nought for me discovers who he is" (Mt 10:39b). Lord, *you* are our life. Turn us to you and keep us there!

Learning About Gentleness Zec 9:9-10
Rom 8:9, 11-13
14th Sunday   A Mt 11:25-30

What strange quirk in us will not allow us to accept the Lord as gentle and kind? For some reason we want to be afraid of God, to fear his judgment, to be nervously sensitive about sinning, to be anything but like the loving Mary who could just sit at Christ's feet and humbly rejoice in his nearness.

The Lord gives us plenty of signs of his gentleness. He did not spring into this world fully armed and ready for battle; he came as an infant. He did not rule like Herod; he ruled by washing his apostles' feet. He had no desire to be a political and avenging savior of Israel; he wanted just to bring the Father's kingdom to full growth. He did not conquer by battles and by killing others; he won by allowing himself to be killed. And in today's Gospel he says it as plainly as he can: "I am gentle and humble of heart" (Mt 11:29a).

Lord, you will not drive anyone. You will not force or hurt or degrade or destroy anyone. You merely want others to share your peace, your happiness, your awareness of the reality of your Father. You invite us all to learn from you, to come to you with our weary burdens and find refreshment.

When you speak like that, why do we refuse to hear you? It would be so much to our advantage. Yet, when we are hurt or discouraged, lonely or bitter or angry we seek distraction in movies or TV; we do anything to relieve the pain in our hearts except to turn to you.

There you stand, Lord, unheeded. And there we go still uncured and perhaps doubly burdened, because we have not sought the one friend who can heal us. Lord Jesus, you are as close as prayer. Help us to allow you to bear our crosses.

The Ripening Word Is 55:10-11
Rom 8:18-23
15th Sunday   A Mt 13:1-23

We may take our families for a ride into the green and golden countryside. There we will see fields ripening for harvest, fields that we remember as brown and dead only a few months ago. How lovely it is when ripening life graces the world, and how miraculous the transformation! A little sun and rain, the good earth, a tiny seed—and life springs up where once there was sterility.

The Lord's eyes looked on that miracle too. And he saw a sign of the way the Father works when he deals with human beings. All he asks is a good earth, an open and receptive person. He will provide the sun and the rain, the sermons, books and people, the joys or the sorrows of everyday life. Above all he sends the seed, his Word, in Jesus Christ. The Scriptures, the Church and the sacraments continue his presence among us. *That* presence has more power than the growing seed which shatters a sidewalk in a young plant's relentless push towards full life.

Lord, your Father wants us to have full life. He has planted his seed in our hearts. Left to itself in the goodness of our hearts, that seed will grow and transform us until nothing evil remains within us. It will bear fruit brought to maturity in the Holy Spirit: in our joy, our peace, our zeal, our love, our kindness, our firmness, our gentleness.

Lord, Isaiah says in today's reading: "[My word] shall not return to me void" (Is 55:11b). Indeed it shall not. Keep us open to it, make us treasure it, bring it to full fruitfulness in us. Lord, only our hardness of heart can frustrate it. Be stronger than us, Lord, and make us ready for your Father's harvest.

Practicing Tolerance Wis 12:13, 16-19
Rom 8:26-27
16th Sunday   A Mt 13:24-43

Thank goodness that tolerance is more honored among us than it used to be. We no longer emblazon an adultress with the scarlet letter. We are able to work with Methodists and Lutherans and Episcopalians. We have made progress in discovering that the person who is not against us stands besides us.

But the Lord also said, "He who is not with me is against me" (Lk 11:23a). He had the wisdom to know when to be tolerant and when to be firm.

We sometimes stumble in our attempts to be both tolerant and firm at the right times. We who are fathers and mothers love our children deeply, and we give thanks for the gift of that love. It has brought us much happiness. But it can also hurt. When a son turns from the Church we love, are we to disown him, fight with him, reason with him, or wait for him to return? When a daughter runs away, or gets pregnant, or wants to marry a boy whose whole destiny is etched with disaster, what are we to do? We don't know. Neither are our children free from confusion. Although they no longer say, "Don't trust anyone over 30," they sometimes act out that principle.

Lord, we need your prudence and your love, especially when our wills clash with the wills of those we love. Teach us what to do. Tolerance is a tricky virtue; we desperately need your help if we are to practice it well.

As You Would Have It 1 Kgs 3:5, 7-12
Rom 8:28-30
17th Sunday   A Mt 13:44-52

That was quite an invitation given in today's first reading: "Ask something of me, and I will give it to you" (1 Kgs 3:5b). Solomon asked for an understanding heart, and that pleased God. It would be an interesting thing if that invitation were offered to each one of us. Many stories have toyed with variations of the idea: the genie in the lamp, the fairy godmother, the mysterious donor of a million dollars.

What would we ask for? It would probably be something we hold deeply within our hearts. Would it be long life, or health, or a peaceful and loving home,

or a job that would settle all our problems? The Lord
once said that our hearts stay with our treasure. Maybe
we could reverse that and say, "Where our heart is, there
we want our treasure to be." Knowing what we would
ask for could help us learn so much about what we
really hold dear.

Lord, how wonderful it would be if we asked, as
you did in Gethsemane, for the fulfillment of the
Father's will. We might be frightened to go that far,
because we see what happened to you.

But, Lord, that's where we are so stupid—we *do
not* see what happened to you. We see the cross, but we
do not see the resurrection. We see you bloody and
dead, but we must have faith in you glorious and immortal. The Father did not stop at your death. He wanted
something more for you. And he does not want our
suffering or death either. He wants us gloriously alive
forever.

So why are we so afraid to say, "Do with me as
you want"? The old martyr had it right: "For 84 years
he has always treated me well. I will not deny him
now." The Father always loves us, no matter what. Lord
Jesus, help us to trust him.

Looking for Bargains Is 55:1-3
Rom 8:35, 37-39
18th Sunday   A Mt 14:13-21

Why spend your money for what is not bread;
 your wages for what fails to satisfy?
(Is 55:2a)

Most of us would nod our heads in agreement; we
have worked hard and we have no wish to squander our
paycheck on foolishness. Most of us look for full value
for our dollars. We know where the bargains are, and we
take advantage of them as long as we are sure that we
will be satisfied. Isaiah says something that we accept as

nothing more than common sense.

But of course Isaiah refers to more than just a trip to the supermarket. He has something much more crucial in mind. His thoughts reflect the Lord's mind. Jesus once praised the initiative of the worldly. Worldlings know the value of what they want and are willing to spend to get it. The trouble is that they don't want enough. Give them a house, a car, a good job, a couple of children, some friends and some power, and they seem not to want much else.

But the Lord challenges the pursuit of the world at the cost of self-destruction. Even when we protest that we seek less than the whole world, his word still has a hard edge. His command is to love God with all our heart, soul and strength, and to love our neighbor with the same intensity with which we provide for ourselves.

When we are worldly, Lord, we are shrewd, perhaps even wise; but our wisdom is the subtlety of a person who can move checkers skillfully around a board. We know how to keep a step or so ahead of the rest and how to capitalize on somebody else's mistakes.

But, Lord, let us raise our eyes from the checkerboard. You have given us just so much time on this earth, and just so many talents to make our stay here worthwhile. Don't allow us to waste ourselves on things that never satisfy us deeply and ultimately.

A Whispered Presence 1 Kgs 19:9, 11-13
Rom 9:1-5
19th Sunday   A   Mt 14:22-33

We quickly turn to the Lord when tragedy or sorrow or turmoil disrupts our life. When cancer invades our own bodies or attacks someone we love, the phrase that comes automatically to our lips is, "Pray for me," or, "Remember my friend at Sunday Mass." Deaths, sicknesses, operations and disasters—all these things turn our minds to the Lord, and we pray for help in carrying our cross. And we are wise to ask his help in crises, because, like Peter, our instinct warns us that we may drown if we do not ask for help.

But we can also learn from Elijah's experience in today's first reading. The Father taught him something we of the 20th century also desperately need: that God is not to be found only in moments marked by turbulence and turmoil. We don't have to feel our feet slipping into the depths before we have the right to call on the Lord. Those moments are, thankfully, comparatively rare in our life. Moments of peace, of routine, even of boredom, usually form the fabric of our whole day. Eight hours of work followed by supper with the family and an evening watching TV or helping the children with homework are much more familiar to us than those unsettling times when the pattern is broken by the unusual.

Lord, you are there in those quiet moments, and you ask that we see you there and thank you and praise you for always being Emmanuel, God-with-us. No moment passes when you do not stand at our door and knock. No moment exists in which you are not present to us.

Lord Jesus, help us to see you in the peace of a quiet evening at home, in the smile of our spouse, in the gentle sleep of our children. Let us hear you, Lord, even when you whisper.

Irrevocable Gifts

20th Sunday   A

Is 56:1, 6-7
Rom 11:13-15, 29-32
Mt 15:21-28

Once in a while our way of reacting to our children causes us concern. Whether we are parents, priests or teachers, we are sometimes deeply disappointed in the behavior of our children. Their grades are not always as high as they should be; they sometimes stay out an hour beyond the deadline we set. Whenever they slip, we want them to know that they need to improve. And so we punish them. But the way we punish is sometimes cause for concern.

Sometimes we withdraw our love from them; or at least we are such good actors that they interpret our response that way. We become silent with them. We will not allow them to apologize. We make them strangers in our midst for a day or so. And, of course, we win. The children, especially if they are young, are soon eager to be in our good graces again. And when we eventually allow them a smile it is granted as a kind of release from exile. We have won, but we and our children have paid an awful price.

The price is this: We fathers and mothers, priests and teachers have not acted like God our Father. Our children learn what the Father is like by living with us. It is up to us to do his work in our own little worlds. St. Paul tells us today what God is like: "God's gifts and his call are irrevocable" (Rom 11:29).

Lord, we never have to win back your Father's love when we sin. It is always there; all we have to do is to claim it. When we turn back to him, he is already rushing toward us. He does not know what it is to make us pay for his love. How *could* we pay for it? We have nothing, Lord, that is not already a gift from him.

Lord, the gift of life we give our children is also irrevocable. Let our love be just as faithful. Let us be to our children as our Father is to us.

Who Do You Say That I Am?   Is 22:15, 19-23
                                       Rom 11:33-36
21st Sunday   A   Mt 16:13-20

Every Sunday, we go to the altar and there receive the bread that has become the Lord himself. If any time exists for total honesty with him, it is that moment. Hypocrisy is foolish; why put up any kind of front? He sees through us, and he knows us better than anyone else ever will. But perhaps it is wise to remind ourselves not to put on an act with him, because at moments like these we sometimes find ourselves using inflated language that we otherwise never use and faking emotions we don't really feel.

What would be our honest answer to the question the Lord put to Peter: "Who do you say that I am?" (Mt 16:15b)? Peter called him "the Messiah . . . the Son of the living God!" (Mt 16:16). That was quite an answer. It expressed an inward yearning of Peter that said, "You are everything I or my people have ever wanted." What would our answer be?

> Sometimes, Lord, you really are the person around whom everything, absolutely everything, revolves. We could not live a day without prayer to you; we could not make a decision without appealing to you; we could not love without including you; and when we sin, all we want to do is to return to you. Yes, Lord, sometimes we know you are our savior, our friend, our brother, our God.
>
> But at other times, honesty would make us admit that you are not that central in our life. Then we are the losers, but only until we recognize that we are losers. For you, Lord, never cease being the savior, friend, brother and God of each one of us every minute of our lives. We don't have to win you, Lord. All we have to do is recognize that we have been won by you. Lord, help us to say: "You are *my* Lord and God."

A Harsh Lesson

Jer 20:7-9
Rom 12:1-2
Mt 16:21-27

22nd Sunday   A

In last week's Gospel Peter was praised for his act

of faith, and rewarded by being made the bedrock of
the Church. This week he is named a satan for judging
not by God's standards but by man's. And Peter accepted
the correction. But we can still feel a little sorry for
him. After all, he loved Jesus so much, and when Jesus
predicted his death at the hands of the Jewish leaders,
Peter wanted to spare the Lord the agony he foresaw.
Even Jesus, when that agony was upon him, prayed to
the Father not to allow it if it could be avoided. So
Peter could not have been wicked in his urging: "May
you be spared, Master!" (Mt 16:22b). Most of us would
have said the same thing.

We still struggle with suffering. Not many of us
understand our own sufferings, much less the troubles
that plague the Church. We see Christians persecuted in
the Eastern European countries, and we think that God
is cursing them. But perhaps he is not. Perhaps the cross
they bear is the weight not of their own sins but the
weight of the apathy and laziness of us who find our
untroubled hour in church each week a chore we hurry
to finish. The old truth still holds: "The blood of the
martyrs is the seed of the Church." Out of love, those
persecuted believers carry the burden of our failure.

**Readiness to suffer and to love—how much we still
need to follow you in that commitment. Lord, the only
thing that kills the Church is lukewarmness. The only
thing that kills each one of us as Christians is a radical
unwillingness to suffer and to love. Sometimes you have
to teach us that lesson harshly. But, please, Lord, never
stop teaching it.**

A Delicate Business

Ez 33:7-9
Rom 13:8-10
Mt 18:15-20

23rd Sunday   A

We do not always find it easy to keep the Lord in
exact focus. We cannot see him, and unless we have the

healthy habit of reading his Word daily, we hear him only once a week or so. We are so easily led into hearing only what pleases us in what he says, and we can conveniently forget his hard sayings. And yet the hard sayings are just as necessary for us. Our hearts grow warm when we hear him say that his yoke is easy, his burden light. But we tune out his command to take up our cross and follow in his steps.

That is why we might be uneasy when we hear today: "If your brother should commit some wrong against you, go and point out his fault" (Mt 18:15a). A lot of us would rather suffer the wrong in silence and give Christ as a reason. After all he did tell us to turn the other cheek. Besides, we know the scourge the world endures in those who think that their great mission in life is to correct everybody else. Such people have succeeded where Adam failed: They have made themselves like gods.

This whole business of rebuke and correction is very delicate, and perhaps it can never be done well except by those who really believe that the Lord is present wherever his people gather.

Lord, when my brother and I love you and he hurts me, I can mention my pain to him, and in you we will both find peace. But, Lord, if I rebuke only out of my self-righteousness and my hurt pride, all I have done is to take the knife from my brother's hands, not to cure but to kill.

Lord Jesus, stay with us. We are so human, especially when we have been hurt. If we cannot immediately forgive, let us, Lord, at least be willing to talk it over.

Doubly Wounded

24th Sunday   A

Sir 27:30—28:7
Rom 14:7-9
Mt 18:21-35

Again this week we struggle with a hard saying. We must forgive one another from our hearts, lest hatred and the desire for revenge boil up within us like an infection.

It is amazing how doubly wounding a harsh word or an act of disloyalty to us can be, or an enemy's glee at our misfortune or mistake. Any demonstration of ill-will towards us lacerates us; and there we have one wound, a wound inflicted on us by someone else. But we seem to have the unfortunate power of inflicting a second wound on ourselves *by* ourselves. Paul referred to this second kind of wound when he told the Corinthians that love does not brood over injuries.

The terrible thing about hatred and revenge is the double harm they cause. They can cripple the person on whom the revenge is taken. Even more, they cripple the avenger, because hatred is not and never will be the climate in which our health can flourish. The revengeful always carry a double-bladed knife. They can never run it through someone else without its also piercing their own hand. In the end, revenge is never sweet.

So, Lord, let us think of the last person who kicked us or defrauded us, hated us or laughed at us. Did we want to get even? If we did, was it sweet? And if it was, did bitterness soon follow? Lord Jesus, help us, because none of your teaching on this topic is easy!

Unexpected Choices

25th Sunday   A

Is 55:6-9
Phil 1:20-24, 27
Mt 20:1-16

It is easy to believe Isaiah when he tells us that God's ways and thoughts are not our ways of acting or thinking. All we have to do is to look at the Father's dealings with the chosen people to understand.

He did not select a powerful nation to be his elect; he chose a race of slaves. He did not delegate someone who had lived the slaves' lot to deliver them; he appointed a man who was raised in the luxury of Pharaoh's court. He consistently selected younger brothers to rule older ones: Jacob over Esau; Joseph over his jealous brothers; David the young shepherd over his older and more mature brothers. Saint Paul believed that God chose the weak of the world to confound the strong; he even said that he, Paul, gloried in his weakness so o that God's power could be manifested.

Indeed, the history of God's dealings with his people show him doing things in strange and unexpected ways. We should be used to his ways by now.

And yet, Lord, we are not. We still find your parable today about the owner's way of paying his workers difficult to accept. We would not have used the owner's technique; we would have done everything possible to preserve our reputation for being completely just. And we hardly pattern our wage structure after his. Still, the point you made about the owner, your Father, is admirably served by the parable: He does not treat us only with justice; he treats us always with incredible generosity.

Or, Lord, we look at the suffering in our own lives and we wonder why your Father has turned from us. But of course he has not, no more than he turned from you in your suffering. We seem to expect that your Father's love always should come as consolation. But you show that it also comes as a cleansing and burning fire.

Lord, we do not always find it easy to transfer the clear teaching of the Bible into an acceptance of the life the Father actually gives us. Help us, Lord, to grow into a more perfect understanding that the Father always blesses, even when we are hurting. Let us always remember that everything he does comes from an infinitely generous and fatherly love. Let us not judge his ways by ours.

The Consequences of Belief

26th Sunday   A

Ez 18:25-28
Phil 2:1-11
Mt 21:28-32

When the Lord looks into the depths of each one of us, he must see an amazing variety of responses to his invitation to follow him. Some of us are willing, but the responsibilities of job and household are so heavy right now that we can't yet find the time for him. Others are held back by a sinful pleasure too sweet to give up. Still others hesitate for fear of standing apart from the crowd. So many responses, and so few of them what the Lord waits to hear. But occasionally one of us will say, "Yes, Lord," and really mean it. Occasionally one who has said no thinks better of that ungracious word.

The question asked of Simon Peter is still the most important one in the world: "Who do you say that I am?" (Mt 16:15b). And that question is not only for Peter; it is for every one of us—everyone. And everyone must answer individually for himself or herself. When our answer is spoken with Peter's sincerity, then consequences will follow for us as they did for him. For Peter's answer proclaimed Jesus Messiah, Son of the living God, and he later died for that conviction. What are our answers? What might the consequences of our belief turn out to be?

Lord, you ask us to believe so vitally that even if every neighbor 10 blocks around were to make fun of you, we could still proclaim you the Messiah. You ask a personal question of each one of us, and you wait for a personal response. Help us to make it with our hearts, our hands, our lips, our whole life. Our belief in you is never without consequence.

In Spirit and in Truth

27th Sunday   A

Is 5:1-7
Phil 4:6-9
Mt 21:33-43

We have seen in the countryside the hard work of farmers in preparing the soil, sowing and weeding, fertilizing and harvesting. We sense the anxiety of these laborers as they see their crops ripen, and we can appreciate their anguish when crops are blighted by drought or too much rain or insects. The prophet Isaiah had the farmers of his day in mind when he described the complaints of the vinegrower against his barren vines.

But Isaiah also had in mind another vinegrower and another vine: God and the people he had nurtured ever since Moses. In some mysterious way the Father has the same heartache as the unsuccessful farmer when we do not produce. That's both frightening and exhilarating. We human beings have such a hold on the heart of God that he is never satisfied until we are fruitful.

What fruit does the Lord expect from his vineyard? A people who will worship in spirit and in truth (cf Jn 4:23a). He grieves when his people pay homage with their lips while their heart is elsewhere (cf Mt 15:8). He tends his vineyard at Sunday worship, nourishing it with prayer and song, with his word and his flesh. He gives so much to us, and he waits for a personal response. And he expects something worthwhile.

Lord, if all our prayer comes from our lips, touch us now so that we may redeem our acts of worship. If, though, in all truth and with our whole spirit we have been saying, "My Lord and my God," we thank you and praise you. May we go forth to serve you in our family, our friends and our work. Lord, help us to keep our spirit truthful!

Not Too Different

28th Sunday   A

Is 25:6-10
Phil 4:12-14, 19-20
Mt 22:1-14

The Lord has gone ahead of us to prepare a place in his Father's house (cf Jn 14:2). Of that house, St. Paul wrote: "Eye has not seen, ear has not heard... what God has prepared for those who love him" (1 Cor 2:9b).

Our trouble is that we have to *imagine* the heaven prepared for us, and we are not very good at making images. The most familiar are not that exciting: fluffy clouds, wings, halos and harps. The prophet Daniel pictured the Ancient of Days in awesome majesty, and John portrayed Jesus as the Lamb in the heavenly Jerusalem. But even those images can leave us cold. We don't write that kind of literature any more.

The problem with such pictures is that they show heaven as too different from the world we know. We would be strangers there, searching in vain for a few homey and familiar features. But heaven must be very familiar if the Lord can say it is already in our midst (cf Lk 17:21)—as familiar as the depths within us where we encounter our very selves.

The deepest secret of trying to understand heaven is contained in the Lord's statement: "Where two or three are gathered in my name, there am I in their midst" (Mt 18:20). Heaven is not so much a place as it is a set of relationships. It opens before us when we accept the Lord as the most important person in our lives, when we open our hearts to the power of the Spirit who binds all in love.

Heaven, Lord, is as familiar to us as family. Forever and ever we will be at home in the Father's house, and he will dance in exuberance over our coming. That kind of heaven, Lord, we can understand. We have already glimpsed it around our supper tables. It's great, Lord. We want more of it!

Enduring Fidelity Is 45:1, 4-6
1 Thes 1:1-5
29th Sunday   A   Mt 22:15-21

Now the Church year winds down to its close. Looking back over the long stretch of weeks since the first Sunday of Advent, we can see the seasons of happiness and sorrow. Through it all we have endured, and for that we give thanks to God.

A prayer like that makes sense. For human beings, endurance over a long expanse of time is no small virtue. It's one that we desperately need, because it makes us so much like the Father. If any quality of his is stressed in Scripture, it is his fidelity. No matter how many times we are unfaithful, he is everlastingly faithful to us. He will never stop being our Father. He is so committed to us that he will never break the bond. Only we have the terrifying power to disown our own Father.

For another year we have endured. St. Paul's words reassure us: "...we constantly are mindful before our God and Father of the way you are proving your faith, and laboring in love, and showing constancy of hope in our Lord Jesus Christ" (1 Thes 1:3).

Lord, we have tried to be faithful. Once in a while we have weakened, played the prodigal. Still we gather in your name, to pray and sing with our lips and our hearts. Here, Lord, is where we belong. Here life makes sense. Root us faithfully in you, for you are our peace and our joy.

Bless our day-by-day life, our family ups and downs, our hours of work, our constant preoccupations. Through them and in them we try to find you. And you are there. Lord, thank you for *never* leaving us!

With Our Whole Heart

30th Sunday   A

Ex 22:20-26
1 Thes 1:5-10
Mt 22:34-40

We hear the basis of all the Old Testament texts today. Jesus says:
"You shall love the Lord your God
with your whole heart,
with your whole soul,
and with all your mind." (Mt 22:37)
We wonder how possible it is for us to obey. If a commandment cannot be obeyed, especially one that is at the base of everything else, we are indeed in trouble. But it would be so unlike the Father to command the impossible. We have to ask what he really wants.

When we look at the cross, we see that God allowed Christ's death, and we are not sure we have the strength to endure such suffering. But we also look at the serene lives of people like St. Bede the Venerable who spent almost his whole life in a monastery, and we see that it is not death the Father commands, but life. All he wants is that we live as Jesus did.

But we wonder even if that kind of life is possible for us. Christ wandered free, unconcerned with job or family or home. Most of us are burdened with all these preoccupations. How can we love God with all our mind when our mind is absorbed with worries about the children's education? But then we think of the astonishing fact that *no one* has exactly reproduced the Lord's life. But he did not come to save no one. He came to save everyone. So each one must be able to fulfill the great commandment in his or her own way. Our Father is not cruel.

Perhaps, Lord, the key to how to love your Father undividedly is already in our hand. Welcoming our children into our lives has not divided our love, but multiplied it. The gift of friendship is a gift of wholehearted love. In fact, Lord, how can anybody love halfheartedly? Love is always with the whole heart! So, Lord Jesus, our request today is this: Let our love always be whole, no matter how often we give it away.

In Love and Freedom　　　　　Mal 1:14–2:2, 8-10
　　　　　　　　　　　　　　　　1 Thes 2:7-9, 13
31st Sunday　A　　　　　　　　Mt 23:1-12

　　　Today's reading make us face the uncomfortable fact that religion can sometimes become divorced from love. In the first reading, Malachi is harsh in his condemnation of religious leaders who wield power without love. In the Gospel the Lord echoes his tone. No one could fault the religious leaders of Christ's day with lack of zeal or even with lack of personal dedication. They applied the law scrupulously to others and to themselves. But they applied it without love. They had forgotten—or never understood—that every smallest law in their code was there to allow freedom to love God and neighbor wholeheartedly. They had made the law of freedom into an intolerable system of chains.
　　　The temptation before which these leaders fell is not absent from us today. It never will be. Piety and religion and wholehearted love are not, unfortunately, always the same thing. They can and should be, but people perversely continue to separate them. We see priests whose ministries have become ecclesiastical ladders, who fashion everything they do in the light of a crozier and miter. We see religious who have made their supposed lives of service into egocentric exhibitions of self-fulfillment.

　　　Lord, these leaders are human, and so are the rest of us. The temptations in their hearts are not so exclusively theirs that we cannot feel them in our hearts as well. When we want to cast stones at our priests and religious, remind us that we are not without sin.
　　　All of us, Lord, priests, religious, laypersons, can be pious without being loving, can be churchgoers with-

out being humble servants, can relish being called good Catholics without being what you really want us to be. Lord Jesus, straighten us out! Make our piety show loving and humble hearts!

Come, Lord Jesus!

32nd Sunday   A

Wis 6:12-16
1 Thes 4:13-18
Mt 25:1-13

Close now to the end of the Church year, we hear the Lord's warning to be ready for him wherever and whenever we may encounter him. The Scriptures speak of his Second Coming, an event of joy and triumph. We have to admit that our waiting for Christ to come and claim his victory has lost the urgent expectation of his first followers. When the early Church prayed, "Come, Lord Jesus!" they really expected to see him appear on the clouds at any moment. For better or worse, we no longer have that thrilling expectation. We have grown accustomed to waiting.

Our long experience, though, has not been wasted. We have learned to look for the Lord at every turn. We know he will come for us at the end of life, and so death is a much less distressing prospect than it might otherwise be. We know he comes to us to pour his Spirit into our hearts, nurturing there the growth of his Kingdom. We find him in our midst whenever we gather in his name. We meet him in the poor, the stranger, the prisoner. He touches us in every sacrament, the signs of his presence among us. Bread and wine, water and oil herald his coming.

We have not lost everything in our dimmed expectation of his final triumph. We know it will happen, but we have grown wiser in allowing its time to be determined by the Father—that is what Jesus suggested anyway.

Perhaps, Lord, we have grown wiser in faith to

search for you in the faint whispers by which you so often steal in among us. We expect you not only at your Second Coming or the unknown moment of our death, but at every minute of our lives. You always stand at the door and knock.

Open our ears, Lord. Do not allow us to miss you. Do not let our preoccupation with ourselves and our concerns deafen us to your constant presence. Lord, help us to welcome you now and always.

Not Ours Alone to Keep Prv 31:10-13, 19-20, 30-31
1 Thes 5:1-6
33rd Sunday   A Mt 25:14-30

Often during this year we have prayed that the Lord might make us what he wants us to be. But today's readings make us reflect that he can do only so much for us. He can offer us every gift he has, but if we keep our face turned away and our hands closed, he is stopped. We have a terrifying power to say no to him, and sometimes we are foolish enough to exercise it.

Most of us do try to open our eyes to see the Lord, to open our hands to receive his gifts. Even here, though, we must be alert to what the readings say today: After we become aware that he has saved us and that we have received the gift of his risen life, he expects us to do something with his gift. We must not clutch his gift to our breast as if the treasure was meant for us alone. It was indeed meant for us—but not for us *alone*.

The Scriptures tell us we must give as a gift the gift we have received. If we clutch it to ourself or bury it in the ground, we have every chance in the world of losing it. No, the Lord's gift, like himself, is never content to lie dead in the earth, for the simple reason that his gift is life and love. Life always wants to propagate itself. God made it that way. And love is meaningless without an object.

Lord, you expect a return on the investment you have made in us. You have left the completion of your work in our hands. Don't let us be lazy, Sunday-morning-only Catholics, obligations-only Catholics, avoidance-of-sin Catholics. Don't allow us to clutch your gift to ourselves and offer it to no one else. Lord, bring us all to the generosity of giving what we have received. Help us to see that giving does not make us poor. It opens up your treasure to us even more!

His Kind of Kingdom

Ez 34:11-12, 15-17
1 Cor 15:20-26, 28
Mt 25:31-46

34th or Last Sunday of the Year
Christ the King   A

We thank and praise the Lord for telling us how he will judge us! The Father has given all judgment into his hands, and he could have chosen to be severe and demanding. He could have made us subject to a code even more severe than the one given to Moses; after all, Moses was only a man acting as a messenger for God. Jesus is more. He is God-himself-made-man. And if things were hard under Moses, they could have been infinitely harder under him. But they are not; they are so much simpler and deeper. That's not to say that they are not difficult. They are, but all the Lord demands springs from the best and most profound instincts built within us for happiness. Our foolishness sometimes blinds us to those instincts, but they are there.

What is our instinct when we see the pinched, hungry face of a starving child? We want to do something, and we can become angry at the circumstances that cause any child to go hungry. Or we see a poor woman coming to Church week after week in a tattered coat; so many of us feel pity and would like to help her. It's the next step that is so important. Pity without action is a kind of painful pleasure. But when we act on our instinct and feed the child or send a coat to the woman, we begin to know happiness.

When we follow our hearts, Lord, an amazing thing happens. We find that we have done your will; and not only have we done what you would have done, we actually have done it to you. You came to serve; imitating you, we serve you—even when you are not in our minds at all.
How could you have made things any simpler? All we have to do is to listen to your call to our best selves, and you are our reward forever and ever. Lord Jesus, this is your kind of kingdom. It makes a lot of sense.

Cycle B

Being On Guard Is 63:16-17, 19; 64:2-7
1 Cor 1:3-9
1st Sunday of Advent   B Mk 13:33-37

On this first Sunday of Advent, let us heed the Lord's advice to "Be on guard" (Mk 13:37). The Gospel directs his words beyond the circle of his hearers; they are meant for us as well. Jesus wants us to be alert, to be watchful for his coming. Even as we wait for his coming at the end of the world, he steals into our midst in many ways. For many of these "little comings," we are most definitely not on guard.

He pledged his presence wherever two or three gather in his name. Only two need speak his name as they vow a lifetime love, and a household is filled with his presence through the years. He is there to share all a family's joys and tears, there to break bread at every meal—unnoticed.

A handful of people struggle into church to celebrate his presence in the Eucharist. But even as they wait for the liturgy to begin, the Lord has slipped into the pews. Wandering minds miss his coming; careless eyes are blind to the rich possibilities of a Christian get-together.

And when Mass ends, his companions will race to the door without him, or busy themselves with coats and kids during the closing hymn. If the Lord were to die again at the hands of his people, it could well be in the church parking lot.

Lord, keep us on guard. Make us sensitive to your presence among us. Let us see you in our families,

around our tables. Let us welcome you with warmth
and joy in all our parish gatherings. Please, Lord, open
our sleepy eyes this Advent.

The God of Compassion   Is 40:1-5, 9-11
                             2 Pt 3:8-14
2nd Sunday of Advent   B   Mk 1:1-8

    Isaiah speaks with a compassionate tenderness in
today's first reading. When he first spoke his message, it
was meant for despairing exiles in Babylon. But Isaiah
also speaks to us today. And many of us need to hear
his message, especially as Christmas draws closer and we
prepare for an Advent confession: "Now is the time to
rejoice in the mercy of the Lord; he has punished you
long enough. Now he wants to comfort you."
    Some of us do need that message. Perhaps we have
been wrecking our marriages by letting our desires wander.
And we have been punished by the misery in our
own consciences and the unhappiness in the eyes of our
spouses and children. Today Isaiah invites us to be cured
of all that pain, to see where our peace and happiness
are, and to come back again to the care of the Father.
    Or perhaps some of us have lost the meaning of our
work and drift listlessly from day to day, happy only on
payday, and doing as little as possible to earn our pay.
But all that is so joyless. We can never be satisfied with
a life whose meaning is marked out in dollar bills. We
need more and we want more, and we know it. And on
this point Isaiah also speaks to us today when he tells us
that the Lord God brings his reward with him—and we
can be sure that God's reward will not be a little piece
of green paper.

    Lord, your Father brings comfort and tenderness,
freedom and peace, strength and joy. He is a Father who
rejoices over us as a father rejoices over a son or daughter about to be married. He is a Father who rushes down

the road to fold us in his arms before we can say, "I'm sorry." He is a real Father, a totally committed Father.

And you, Lord, are his firstborn, inviting us to your happiness. Help us to accept your invitation and to understand where our real happiness is. Grant to us the kind of grace that enlightens and strengthens so that we can say no to all that hurts and destroys ourselves and those we love. Lord Jesus, teach us how to be children of whom your Father can say: "You too are my beloved sons and daughters!"

Preparing for Joy　　　　　　　　Is 61:1-2, 10-11
　　　　　　　　　　　　　　　　　　1 Thes 5:16-24
3rd Sunday of Advent   B　　　　　Jn 1:6-8, 19-28

We are now very close to our celebration of the Lord's birth into our world. City streets and shopping malls glitter now with tinsel, trees and lights. We have watched the children become more and more excited by expectations of the big day. And we have listened to the carols that fill the air. No other time of the year is prepared for quite so completely as Christmas.

That's why it is so good to hear the readings of today's liturgy. St. Paul calls us to rejoice; should we not? We celebrate the nearness of Jesus, our joy and our salvation. Isaiah joins Paul in anticipating the joy that the Lord will bring. Together they invite us to be sure that our preparation for Christmas is complete in every way.

For glitter and tinsel, music and lights, the excitement in the eyes of children make sense only when they emerge from hearts filled with the joy of today's Scripture. It was Jesus for whom John the Baptist prepared; it is Jesus for whom we must prepare. Our Christmas is not to be a day whose center is the gifts we give; it must be a day whose center is the gift we have been given in Jesus Christ.

When Jesus is the cause of all our joy, then let our hearts brim over with happiness. Then let us love one another in the gifts we offer, in the visits we make, in the carols we sing.

You are the joy of our soul, Lord Jesus. Everything you do is good. You want to help the poor, comfort the sorrowing and free us from every sort of bondage. You want your world to be a place of justice and praise. No wonder you can make us so joyful, Lord. You want to take away everything that causes sorrow. And so we cry today: Come, Lord Jesus, come!

The Impossible Made Real 2 Sm 7:1-5, 8-11, 16
Rom 16:25-27
4th Sunday of Advent   B Lk 1:26-38

We are very close now to our celebration of Jesus' birthday. It is well to pause and reflect on what we have been preparing for. We have been through many Christmases, and we truly love the day. But perhaps we will never completely grasp all that the day signifies.

One sentence that Gabriel speaks to Mary in today's Gospel might help us, though, to plunge more deeply into the miracle of Christmas. "Nothing is impossible with God" (Lk 1:37). And indeed nothing is. Not the creation of a universe; not the deliverance of a gaggle of motley Hebrew slaves from their Egyptian masters; not the freeing of an exiled Judean people from their Babylonian captors. In so many cases the Father does what we would humanly judge to be the impossible. He creates and re-creates with a power and a freedom and an ingenuity that show how completely different he is from us who plod and scheme and fail.

And nowhere does he show his power over the impossible more than in Jesus. For Jesus is God. Yet people spoke with him, ate with him, laughed and sorrowed with him—and denied, betrayed and killed him. People simply do not do these things with God. At least that's the way we humans would ordinarily think. In fact, the Hebrews at Mt. Sinai were vehement in insisting that a certain distance be preserved between themselves and God. Therefore they implored Moses to speak to God for them, lest they die.

Lord Jesus, you are the living sign of God's power to do the impossible. In you the frightening, searing, terrifying reality we call God has become one of us, walking among us, drawing us, calling us "little flock," and telling us not to fear. Lord Jesus, we will never understand all the mystery of God-made-man. But help us, as the feast of your human birthday draws near, to be a little more aware of the humanly impossible reality that you are: Immanuel, *God-with-us.*

An Unforgettable Day   Is 62:11-12
                             Ti 3:4-7
Christmas — Mass at Dawn   Lk 2:15-20

What an everlastingly beautiful day today is! It is the Lord's birthday. It is the day prepared by the Father from the beginning of time because he so loved what he had made that he simply could not stay away from it. It is the day desired by the prophets when they foresaw the coming of Emmanuel. It is a day yearned for by Mary for nine long months, one she would remember for the rest of her life.

For how could she forget this day? The wonderful message from the Father had begun a process in her that swept her along all the time Jesus was growing within her. And any mother could describe how wonderful that whole process is. Now, on this day, the time has come for her to see what her body had known so intimately. Jesus is the child of her womb. She could never forget the day of his birth, the manger, the angels, or Joseph standing beside her.

It is well for us to think about Mary on the Lord's birthday, because through her we can get a much clearer idea of what his birthday means to each one of us. For Mary was the first to have the Son of God as an intimate indweller. But she has certainly not been the last. All of us receive him and harbor him at our Baptism and in every Communion we receive. And his Spirit is a constant presence within us, to whom we can turn anytime we wish.

Lord, you had only one physical mother, but you were not using a mere figure of speech when you called all of us your mothers and sisters and brothers. All of us bear you.
On this feast of Christmas, fill our hearts with Mary's great joy. Help us to say yes to your Father as she did. Help us to treasure all the events of our union with you the way she treasured hers—in our hearts and for always. Grant us, on this day when you gave yourself and can refuse us nothing, the peace of Mary's heart as she sees you, holds you and wonders at God's great goodness. Lord, let our Communion with you today be filled with Mary's thankfulness. Then our Christmas, too, will be unforgettable!

A Holy Union Sir 3:2-6, 12-14
Col 3:12-21
Sunday in the Octave of Christmas Lk 2:22-40
Holy Family   B

These days of Christmas are a lovely time for families. We draw together in an especially intense way. We visit grandparents and welcome other family members to our home. This feast of the Holy Family is a great opportunity to reflect on the sacred grouping called the family—not only on the three people we call the Holy Family, but on all our families. Every family is a holy union blessed by God, and perhaps the place where we best see enfleshed Christ's great command to love.
We who are together in families are bound to one

another every hour of every day. We know one another
in a way we know no other persons. We can read one
another's moods and learn to make allowances for one
another's faults. We rejoice in one another's love and
feel our own heart's pride when any member of the
family succeeds.

We know, too, that living under one roof has its
tensions. Every family has to adjust to the imperfections
of every person in it. That's why all of us need to begin
our marriages in and with Christ, and why we want him
to be with us each day. That's why parents and children
need to hear St. Paul's advice in today's second reading:
"Clothe yourselves with heartfelt mercy, with kindness,
humility, meekness and patience" (Col 3:12). It is advice
that makes sense in an intimate group like the family.

**Lord, let your words in all their richness dwell in
us today. For when they are at home in us, we find the
kindness to be merciful and the humility to be meek
and patient. We know we cannot be harsh or proud and
still be at peace with each other. Lord, help all of us to
grow in your wisdom by your grace!**

Slaves No Longer Nm 6:22-27
Gal 4:4-7
Octave of Christmas Lk 2:16-21
Solemnity of Mary, Mother of God

We might wonder sometimes whether we are captured enough by the realities that Paul speaks of in
today's reading. He tells us that we are no longer slaves,
but heirs. Paul implies that slavery is a condition heavily
regulated by law. How one comes to be a slave, how one
lives as a slave, how one can be freed—all these things
demand a set of conventions that clearly set off one person as a master and another as a slave.

Slavery was a matter of law; it was hardly a matter
of love. But sonship was and is a matter of love. It is a
relationship which springs out of an act of love and

should be lived in an atmosphere of love. Laws are left far behind when a good father and a good son live together. Everything that happens in that relationship happens because the two people love each other, and not only because they have obligations to each other.

And so when Paul tells us that we are children of God, he tells us something that should really stagger us. He tells us that we are in a free and easy and comfortable relationship with the awesome God that lets us call him "Father." No more petty regulations; no more chains; no more forced labor. We are not slaves; we are members of the family.

Maybe, Lord, we don't think enough about the kind of family your Father brings us into. We don't reflect on his majesty, his glory, his power, his kindness, his love. We don't know the gift that we have, because we don't know the giver. And so our Catholicism is flat and dead, a matter of do's and don'ts. But you offer us a chance to say "Father" to the most glorious of all realities. Lord, help us to know our dignity and our privilege. Help us to be real sons and daughters of your Father.

Chosen Before the World Began   Sir 24:1-4, 8-12
Eph 1:3-6, 15-18
2nd Sunday After Christmas   Jn 1:1-18

There is a magnificent line in today's second reading: "God chose us in him before the world began" (Eph 1:4a). That's staggering. When Jesus lay in the manger of an inn's outbuilding displaying indifference to all the world's judgments about greatness and power, the Father contemplated him there and was pleased. And he saw us in Jesus.

At least, we were supposed to be there. But were we? The implications of the manger are unsettling if all we want is more money and if all our admiration is for the people with the biggest paychecks. Jesus was at home in the manger. Sometimes we have the feeling we could not be. Our preference is more the king-size bed.

And when Jesus remained in the Temple to speak with the doctors of the Law, the Father saw us in him. He wanted to get started on his Father's work. But he was still only 12 years old, and so he went home with his father and mother to learn more about the human condition. He went and grew in wisdom, age, grace and obedience. In Jesus the Father saw us. Or did he? Are we still growing in real wisdom and open to grace?

Lord Jesus, at your baptism your Father acknowledged you as his beloved Son. And he saw us in you. We too are his beloved sons and daughters. The big difference between you and us, though, is a difference we persist in maintaining: You were sinless. We are not. But we know that your Father loves us despite our sin. And he continues to love us even when we return to sin. But he wants us to be like you. Lord, help us to hate sin. There is no other way to stay with you.

With a Spirit of Adventure

Epiphany

Is 60:1-6
Eph 3:2-3, 5-6
Mt 2:1-12

We don't know very much about the astrologers whom we meet in today's Scripture. St. Matthew tells us that they came from the East, possibly from Babylonia, where the study of the stars was in high honor. But beyond that we do not know how many there were or their names; tradition has supplied those details. But the details are not important. What is important is what these men represent and the spirit in which they acted.

Very simply these men represent all of us who are not Jewish. When these men knelt before the Lord, offering their gifts in worship, all of us Gentiles were there in spirit. We are, as Paul says, "now co-heirs with the Jews" (Eph 3:6a).

On this feast of the Epiphany we kneel before the manger again, and we bless and praise the Lord for including us in the promises given to the Chosen People. And today we offer our own gifts in these favored moments. We offer our contrite and loving hearts.

And today we try to share in the open and generous spirit of the astrologers. Although they knew the heavens, they still responded to the new star when it came to them. They welcomed it and allowed it to lead them away from the familiar and the comfortable. They followed it until it revealed the Lord—and that was quite a prize for their spirit of adventure. Abraham did the same thing, and he earned a limitless family.

Lord, we too are often called to accept the new, to leave the familiar, to search for you in situations and surroundings where we might not have expected to find you. Open us and make us generous. Lord Jesus, we worship you as God-among-us. On this Epiphany day, make us ready for you however you show yourself to us.

A Powerful Sign

Baptism of the Lord   B

Is 42:1-4, 6-7
Acts 10:34-38
Mk 1:7-11

Today's feast is a puzzling one. Even John the Baptizer could not figure out what was happening when Jesus appeared on the banks of the Jordan asking for baptism. He knew the request was backwards. But Jesus insisted, and so John baptized him.

What troubled John, of course, was the nature of the baptism he was giving; he baptized those who were willing to turn away from sin. But he also preached the coming of the Lord, and he knew that the Lord would not have to forsake sin. Jesus came as the enemy of sin. So his baptism might seem useless. Yet Father, Son and Spirit were manifest in that baptism. Jesus made it a

sign of his fundamental stance toward sin. He had no
need to reform; but in him, John's other followers could
see one like themselves standing in opposition to sin.

The Father made this baptism his acknowledgement of Jesus as the blessed servant described by Isaiah
in the first reading. And the Spirit descended to claim
Jesus as his own, and then to lead him into the desert
to fast and pray.

The Lord's baptism was not useless; far from it. It
was a powerful sign of what he was all about: enemy of
sin, only Son of the Father, Messiah anointed by the
Spirit.

**Our own Baptism ought to mean just as much to
us. We too took in Baptism a stance of opposition to
sin. We too were claimed as beloved sons and daughters.
On us also came the Holy Spirit to possess us thoroughly. There, Lord, is where we start to stray. We do not
pray; we do not become workers for the Kingdom. We
allow our Baptism to lie fallow in our life. Lord Jesus,
make us, in this Christmas season, aware of the gifts we
have received in Baptism. Do not let us waste them.**

Beginning With Prayer	Jl 2:12-18
	2 Cor 5:20–6:2
Ash Wednesday	Mt 6:1-6, 16-18

The readings for today's Mass invite us to get
serious about our relationship with the Father. Joel tells
us to turn to God with all our hearts, and Jesus invites
us to make every act of self-sacrifice and prayer and
almsgiving come from so deep within us that we don't
have to have somebody else's approbation to see its
worth. The act will be worthy for the simple reason that
it is an act of wholehearted sorrow for our sin and of
integral love for God.

We need that kind of invitation. Sometimes we
find ourselves becoming halfhearted in our prayer and,

consequently, in all our other ways of loving God and our brothers and sisters. We find prayer slipping out of our lives. Our Masses can become obligations to be fulfilled. Jesus and the Father become almost unreal to us as we fill our lives with the pressures of jobs and families. Overtime, a new baby, troubles with our spouse, or trying for a promotion can preoccupy us to the point where we fall into bed exhausted each night. And when Sunday morning arrives even the hour of Mass can be invaded by the worries of the past week and our plans for the week to come.

Lent is an opportunity to let prayer become a part of our lives. Even 15 or 20 minutes each day with the Lord will do it. We don't have to become monks or nuns. All we have to do is turn our attention to the greatest of all the realities of our life—the Lord. With him we can manage all the other things that clamor for our time. Prayer will not tear us out of our world; it will insert us more deeply into it.

Lord, Lent can be such a blessed time. And so it will be if you help us to begin it in prayer and continue it in discipline and self-sacrifice, so that we can see you again as the conqueror of all the evil in us and around us. We need you so that we can look forward to an Easter celebration of the new life you give us. Lord, above all else, teach us how to live our busy lives with you—not against or without you. You are the joy of our lives. Let us never forget.

Jogging into Lent

1st Sunday of Lent   B

Gn 9:8-15
1Pt 3:18-22
Mk 1:12-15

Most of us can concoct a hundred different ways of putting off a difficult or unpleasant task. We can be ingenious in the delays we create before getting down to the job: a can of beer, a few minutes before the TV, a trip to the store, a chat across the back fence... Suddenly there's no time left to do the job. Our consciences have been cleared by the clock. But, of course, we know deep down the little game we have been playing. And it's a foolish game, if for no other reason than that we have lost the joy of accomplishment. We have done nothing, and nothingness produces bitter fruit.

All of us are now faced with the hard work of Lent. We are being asked to give ourselves to some serious labor, just as Noah and Jesus were. Noah got right to his work; so did the Lord. Jesus followed the Spirit into the desert for a long retreat of prayer and fasting. And when the retreat was over, he knew the kindly touch of the Father through the ministry of his angels.

There are some rewards that are simply unattainable without an outlay of energy. We know that principle when we exercise: a mile or so of jogging will have its effect on us and we'll feel great; but without the sweat we feel no sweetness.

Lord, we know that Lent is hard. But we also know that our spirits are flabby. We have too little of the joy that filled our hearts at Christmas time. So, Lord, on this first Sunday of Lent we want to put ourselves to work. Four days of Lent have already passed, and we have exhausted our excuses. It's time to start.

Lord, help us to pray and do penance for 40 days, to be kind and gentle all our lives. Lord, we need your Easter joy. Help us to prepare for it.

Ready to Respond

2nd Sunday of Lent   B

Gn 22:1-2, 9, 10-13, 15-18
Rom 8:31-34
Mk 9:2-10

Our sympathy with Abraham in today's first reading can go beyond the fact that we understand how great is the gift of a son. The request for Isaac's life was a test not only of Abraham's love for his son; it was a test of something even deeper in him, the ground from which his paternal love grew. We married people especially can sympathize with him, because we too know that kind of testing almost every day of our lives. And maybe we know it even better in our response to each other than in our response to God.

For we see one another every day. We hear the spoken and silent needs of each other. We have vowed to be together until death parts us. But the living of that vow is a minute-by-minute experience, and we now know that what we pledged was a generous and complete openness to each other. We have promised to hold nothing back.

When we pronounced our vows to each other, we pledged a faithfulness that would be proof against the disintegrating forces that would like to tear us apart: the concern for comfort that destroys the willingness to respond to the other's needs; the secretiveness that keeps the other perpetually a stranger; the stunted emotional maturity that sees the other only as a comfort blanket and never as an equal adult.

Marriage, Lord, means two adults coming together to create a world out of their unselfish love. But we can do that only when we have our roots in you.

Abraham's response to you was, "Ready!" (Gn 22:1b). Help us to make the same answer when you call to us in the needs of one another. Openness and readiness are the rich soil in which love grows. Grant us, in this Lenten season, the ability to break down the walls of selfishness that separate us and to hold nothing back.

A Strong and Forceful Man

3rd Sunday of Lent   B

Ex 20:1-17
1 Cor 1:22-25
Jn 2:13-25

Too many times our religious art fails to do the Lord justice. Too often artists depict him as weak and pallid, with hands that could never have handled a workman's tool and a body that is pretty rather than strong. If he were that type of man, then almost everything the Gospels say of him becomes incredible. A weakling does not spend 40 days fasting in a desert; an effeminate man does not draw burly fishermen from their jobs to follow him—and certainly he does not clear out a bustling Temple court.

We don't use our imaginations well when it comes to Jesus. We think his divinity was so apparent that his humanity was almost a needless show. But the plain fact is that his divinity was not that apparent at all. If his "godhead" were so easy to see, the townspeople would not have taken him to the edge of the hill and tried to hurl him to his death. All they saw was a man getting too big for his beginnings. If his divinity were so clear, his people would not have killed him. They wanted to kill a man; they had no intention of killing their God. The Lord could pray for their forgiveness because they did not know what they were doing.

Lord, they did not see all that you were; neither, unfortunately, do we. We do not always see you as the strong, forceful, energetic man that you were. We know you are gentle and tender-hearted, but your meekness and gentleness come from controlled and powerful strength.

Lord Jesus, let us understand you in your strength, your just anger, your human vitality. And when we see injustice and cruelty in our own world, when the time comes for us to be angry, help us to imitate you.

The Experience of Being Lost	2 Chr 36:14-17, 19-23
	Eph 2:4-10
4th Sunday of Lent B	Jn 3:14-21

When as children we wandered away from the familiar street where we lived, we soon found we did not know where we were or how we got there. And we did not like the feelings that surged up in us then: loneliness, fear, longing for someone—anyone—whom we knew. As adults, we can still become completely bewildered on a trip when the map and the reality are at odds; our feelings are amazingly similar to our childhood experience. Of course, when we're older we have resources children don't have. We know we can ask or telephone; we can do something to return us to control over our situation. Still, there are more pleasant experiences than being lost.

We would be wise to recall those feelings on this fourth Sunday of Lent. Today's readings will make sense to us only if we know how lost we have been. Without the Lord, we are lost more completely than a five-year-old 20 blocks from home. We are lost, we have left our home. We not only don't know the way back, but we could not find it if we did. It's as if the father of a very large family had driven his van full of children into the labyrinth of a southern swamp and has no way of getting them out.

Lord, our father Adam did something like that to us. And we, like foolish children, have managed to get ourselves even more thoroughly lost. Only someone who knows the geography of earth and heaven can lead us back home. And you are the one, Lord. You paid dearly for leading us out of our mess. But we will appreciate you only when we see how much of a mess we were in. Lord, give us first a sense of sin, because it is by sin that we wander. And then give us a sense of your mercy. Then, Lord, we will know your salvation.

Etched Into Our Hearts　　　　　　Jer 31:31-34
　　　　　　　　　　　　　　　　　　Heb 5:7-9
5th Sunday of Lent　B　　　　　　　Jn 12:20-33

We are living in the time predicted by Jeremiah—at

least, in part. The prophet speaks of a time when all that is most pleasing to the Father need no longer be commanded. It would be *wanted* far beyond the threshold of law. God's law will be so deeply part of us that it is etched into our hearts, a deep desire to be and do all the Father loves.

We can see the lovely evidence that Jeremiah's prediction is slowly being fulfilled. In the most ordinary of families, the command to love is gently and thoroughly lived. Wives live in love with crippled husbands; husbands tend children whose mothers have too soon been taken by death. Parents sink into senility in the tender care of their middle-aged children.

The same thing is happening in our neighborhoods. People give hours to clean the house of a cancer-stricken friend. They shop for the elderly and call or visit them. Caring people band together to lobby for the unborn; believing people gather in prayer groups to praise the Lord in their midst.

None of these things are commanded. They rise from willing hearts inscribed with God's law, hearts that are generous beyond the demands of any statute. No legislation demands a pot of stew for the old man next door; it is the gift of a loving heart.

Lord, warm our hearts with your love. Let your law be written there. Teach us to pour out our lives in service to each other; ripen in us the rich fruit of care. Let Easter morning find us standing new in your light, ready for the harvest.

A Difficult Attitude Is 50:4-7
Phil 2:6-11
Passion Sunday (Palm Sunday) B Mk 14:1—15:47

St. Paul asks the ultimate of us today: to assume Christ's own attitude. Christ's attitude was one of service; his heart and mind were turned to the needs of others. He was the equal of the Father, yet he made himself the servant of us all. He is the Lord who washed the feet of his disciples.

Even when he was mistreated and put to a shameful death, he continued to serve. Nothing that was done to him erased his love. His attitude was simple and consistent: Son of the God who is love, he loved and will always love. He will never counter hatred with anything but love.

This is the attitude Paul expects us to assume. And we wonder how in the world we can possibly succeed. We know how we feel when we are ignored or cheated, gossiped about or misunderstood. We know that our feelings are not like the Lord's—at least we think we know. But we should pause when we imagine that difference.

Scripture does not present Christ as one who had only pleasant feelings for those who hurt or misunderstood him. He was very direct with Peter when he called him a satan. He spared no words in reference to the hypocrisy of the Pharisees. He showed great pathos when Judas betrayed him in the garden.

Lord, your feelings and your attitudes were not always in harmony. Your feelings in the face of death cried out to be spared, but your attitude was one of submission to the Father's will.

Our feelings, too, tug us in a thousand different directions, not all of them loving or unselfish. Boredom, anger, frustration, bitterness—we feel them all. But, Lord, they need not change our attitude. That we want to be like yours. Like you, we do not find it easy. Lord, help us!

Seeds of Life

Easter Sunday

Acts 10:34, 37-43
Col 3:1-4 or 1 Cor 5, 6-8
Jn 20:1-9

Praise and honor, glory and thanks to God on this Easter Sunday morning! We join Christian believers throughout the world in our worship today because the crucified Lord lives. He has gone into the grip of death, but did not remain there. He has returned from the grave to be with us again, only this time with a life that is the firstfruits of all life, never again to end.

We are the rest of the harvest the Father began when he called Jesus out of the darkness of death. The indestructible seed of immortality within us now pulses with his risen life. He has made us one with him in his death and in his new life.

We celebrate the Lord today—and we also celebrate ourselves, for we have been raised up in his company. Where he is, we are. But in another sense, of course, we are not. The seed of glory is within us, but it needs our physical death before it comes to full flower. While we live our fragile lives for the 60 or 70 years of pregnancy in this womb of our earth, we must grow accustomed to the real life that will be ours.

Lord, we know we still have a debt to pay to our humanity. We know that we shall die. But we also believe that that death is a doorway, a release, an entering into glory. And especially our belief is strong today. It is Easter!

Our death, Lord, will be a birth. Help us to be ready; help us to know where our real home and family and happiness are. Help us to live these few years here with a faith and hope that sees what earthly eyes cannot see and hears that to which bodily ears are deaf. You, Lord, are our life, our destiny and our reward. So again we praise you today as we wish to praise you forever and ever.

A Transforming Faith Acts 4:32-35
 1 Jn 5:1-6
2nd Sunday of Easter   B Jn 20:19-31

We are a week away now from Easter Sunday. And yet we have just begun to celebrate what Easter is all about. Maybe the readings of the Sundays after Easter will deepen our joy in what Jesus has won for us, or maybe we will find them standing in a kind of judgment against us. They then become a kind of insistent invitation to us to become more completely what he has already made us: Christians.

For example, the first reading today tells us of the transformation of life Jesus' first followers experienced. They ceased being selfish and individualistic and materialistic. They discovered that the joy of believing led them into a way of life that opened itself in an incredible generosity to everyone else. Their faith showed itself in love for others. We wonder where we can see some of that same transformation in our own lives.

And in the second reading, John says much the same thing. He tells the early Christians that their faith has given them a new life coming from the depths of God himself; and that new life shows itself in love for everyone else born in the same way. And again we wonder whether we are as aware of that connection as John was.

In the Gospel, Lord, you tell us that not only the first Christians were to have that kind of transforming faith and love. You looked into the long history of people who would call you Lord, and you saw us among them. You called us blessed, because you saw us believing in you even though we do not see you.

But, Lord, maybe you do not see in us all that you want. Maybe we are still too selfish, too individualistic. Maybe this Easter has still not convinced us that faith in you, risen and alive, demands consequences, requires love and generosity at home, at work and in the neighborhood. If so, Lord, let these readings today pierce our hearts. Let us say today with complete conviction: "My Lord and my God." And then lead us to care generously for those with whom we live.

With Confident Hope　　　　　　　Acts 3:13-15, 17-19
　　　　　　　　　　　　　　　　　　1 Jn 2:1-5
3rd Sunday of Easter　B　　　　　　Lk 24:35-48

With trust in the words of St. John, we ask for an increase in hope and confidence. Jesus, he tells us, stands before the Father to plead for us. John's words are addressed to people who know they have sinned, who know they continue to sin.

Many of us have only recently made a Lenten confession. In honesty, most of us would have to admit that what we confessed then we had confessed before. Anger, lying, backbiting, little cruelties to those we love, laziness in our work and cowardice in spreading the gospel—all of these have so often marred our lives. We have confessed them, repeated them, and confessed them again. Sometimes we could almost say to the priest: "Just replay my last confession. I've done it all again."

And yet, we are sorry for all of our sins. We really do want to get rid of the weaknesses we confess. We dare not use the Lord as an absolution machine for sins we have no intention of trying to keep out of our lives.

Lord, we do want to erase our sins; we do not want to write them into our lives again. But they keep slipping back. We turn to you, our intercessor, confident that you will never turn us away. You always receive us and plead before the Father for us.

Lord, all our hope and all our confidence rest in you. Help us to avoid sin. In our weakness, comfort us. You are our Savior, Lord. Increase our confidence in you.

Children of God Acts 4:8-12
1 Jn 3:1-2
4th Sunday of Easter   B Jn 10:11-18

Sometimes we look into our own hearts trying to find there the sense of joyous surprise that shines through John's words:
See what love the Father has bestowed on us
in letting us be called children of God! (1 Jn 3:1).
And too often we find no surprise there at all. And yet that sentence causes the hearts of many people to fill almost to bursting with pride, thankfulness and a profound sense of wonder. "How in the world can this be? Why me? What have I done to deserve all this?"

The answer is nothing. Or almost nothing. In fact, God's children have done every conceivable thing to be sure that they would not deserve his love. They have been adulterers, liars, gossipers, murderers—anything and everything under the sun.

All they need do is be willing to receive. Augustine was no saint before he opened himself to God. He had a mistress and an illegitimate son. But he knew in his own flesh what Paul said about all of us: "While we were still sinners, Christ died for us" (Rom 5:8b). When Augustine recognized that, he started on the way back. And then, at last, that restless craving in his heart for happiness was filled.

Lord Jesus, why do we persist in closing our eyes to our happiness? Why do we stay outside the family circle you want so desperately to draw us into? Why does our proudest title, child of God, mean so little to us? We can rejoice that we were born into the family of Smith or Jones. Why does our being in your family affect us so little?

Lord, we still need to be jolted by you. You have given us so much, but we still need more. We still need the gift of appreciating your gift. Lord Jesus, let *nothing* stand in your way. Finish making us your joyful sisters and brothers.

Pruning for Growth　　　　　　　　Acts 9:26-31
　　　　　　　　　　　　　　　　　1 Jn 3:18-24
5th Sunday of Easter   B　　　　　Jn 15:1-8

Those of us who have fruit trees or rose bushes in our backyard know very well the process the Father works in us. We clip off the dead wood and trim away the sappers so that the plant will not go all to leaf. This attack with shears and hook must seem to an inexperienced observer like a mad assault on the very life of our poor plants. But propelled by our interest in the sweetness of the fruit and the brilliance of the blossom, we know what we're doing: We're bringing the plant to its fullest and most productive life.

The Father does exactly the same thing with us. As St. Irenaeus said, "God's glory is man fully alive." He is infinitely interested in our ripest and most productive life. And so the Father takes shears and pruning hook to us.

We panic. The Father wants the best for us, but trimming and pruning can hurt, and none of us is in love with pain. Besides, we cannot always distinguish what is dead and in need of pruning from what is alive and full of promise. We only feel some part of us being clipped off; only a raw wound remains.

Lord, your Father knows what he is doing, but sometimes, maybe most times, we do not. We get scared and hurt and cry out: "Lord, why me?" Pruning and trimming look and feel, Lord, like wounding and killing. Help us, please, dear Lord, to trust your Father when he takes his shears to us. Out of your Calvary came Easter. It can be that way with us, too. But you must stay by us and help us see.

Headlines About God　　　　　Acts 10:25-26, 34-35, 44-48
　　　　　　　　　　　　　　　　1 Jn 4:7-10
6th Sunday of Easter　B　　　　　Jn 15:9-17

Our newspapers don't always help us understand the view of life St. John speaks of in today's readings. The papers are full of terrorist attacks, wars and murders, of riots and white-collar crime, of floods and fires and wrecks. It is as if bad news is the only *news*. The occasional item about bravery or kindness wears a somewhat surprised air in the midst of its grim neighbors.

But maybe the newspapers don't report the real world. Perhaps they tell us only of the mix-ups, only of the events that are unusual and perverse.

For most of us do not make the front page. We live very quiet lives. We love one person in lifelong fidelity. We fill our homes with peace and our small world with friendliness. We are there to help when sickness or disaster strikes our neighbors. Our days go by, one much like the other, and so we are not very good material for a newspaper story.

Yet, Lord, our lives are real. Our jobs and our families are real. Above all else, our love is real. Our spouses and our children, our relatives and our friends—these people make our lives rich and fruitful. They make our Father more dear and familiar than perhaps we will ever realize on this earth, for he himself is love.

Thank you, Lord, for our quiet love-filled lives which are the real world. Thank you for the likeness of the Father in our hearts. Thank you for the headlines love writes there about God.

Slow Learners　　　　　　　Acts 1:1-11
　　　　　　　　　　　　　　　Eph 1:17-23
Ascension　B　　　　　　　　　Mk 16:15-20

Try to teach a young child something as simple as a

short prayer or the sum of a few numbers. For a few
minutes, you seem to hold his attention. His face is
bright, his eyes wide open. The lesson seems to be getting
through. And then he volunteers something like,
"My tooth fell out," and you clutch your brow and
start all over again.

The apostles put Jesus through that same kind of
experience. For three years, he taught them gently and
patiently, but they were not the most alert of pupils.
Every now and then he must have put his hands on his
hips and shaken his head, wondering how they could be
so dense.

In today's first reading, their lack of perception is
almost comical. The Lord has tried so hard to lead them
to an understanding of his mission. Yet even after his
death they simply could not clear their heads and hearts
of the wish that he would make Israel into a great earthly
power. And so they ask once more: "Lord, are you
going to restore the rule to Israel now?" (Acts 1:6) His
answer: Forget that stuff and finish the much more
valuable and necessary work he has begun.

**Lord, we are very like your apostles. Our grasp of
your message and your mission is not so great either.
Most of us are still struggling with the call to shoulder
our crosses and lose our lives for your sake. The beatitudes
and the command to love one another are challenges
we would rather avoid. But your hard sayings are
as important to us as your words of comfort. Lord Jesus,
open our minds and our hearts to *all* you call us to be.
We are tired of being slow learners!**

Doing Great Things

Acts 1:15-17, 20-26
1 Jn 4:11-16
Jn 17:11-19

7th Sunday of Easter B

The prayer of Jesus is powerful and effective. He
offers himself for the sake of those whom he sends into

the world to fulfill his mission. And his prayer for them
will bear rich fruit. The Lord preached just to the Chosen People, and their leaders had him killed—hardly a
very successful mission. But his apostles infiltrated the
whole Roman world, preaching the gospel with great
success.

We take all of that for granted, perhaps because the
story is so familiar. And yet a most perplexing mystery
is before us. The infinitely expressive Word of God
failed to convey to a people faithful to Mosaic law the
real nature of the lawgiver. But a handful of fishermen
and a tax-collector could step out of a doorway and do
the job after Jesus left them. The power of the Lord's
prayer for them made that possible. He called down the
Spirit on rough and uneducated men, enabling them to
accomplish what he had been sent to do.

Lord, you also prayed for those of us who would
come to faith through the words of your apostles. You
still pray for each of us; you still pour out your Spirit
upon us to enable us, too, to do great things. If we
accomplish nothing, it is not because your prayer has
no power. It is we who will not use the Spirit, will not
open ourselves to him, will not become his avenues of
entrance unto our families and our neighborhoods.
Lord, as Pentecost approaches, open our hearts to the
power of your prayer.

Infinite Love at Work — Acts 2:1-11
1 Cor 12:3-7, 12-13
Pentecost Sunday — Jn 20:19-23

Today we celebrate the *magnalia Dei*, the great
things God has done. For on this day the apostles, once
frightened and defeated men, step out into a city celebrating a great Jewish feast and proclaim the Lord as
risen and alive. And almost as great as *what* they proclaimed was the fact *that* they proclaimed it. They had

every reason to expect the same treatment the Lord had received, and they knew it. That is why they had stayed in hiding. But they did come out, no longer cringing and fearful. They burst out so exuberantly that some of their hearers thought they were drunk. Indeed the Father did great things.

And he still does great things, things we would be wise to think about once in a while. Sometimes we can be so blind. We don't see what the Father is doing in our lives, and so we fail to proclaim his power and to praise and thank him for his unceasing interest in us. We think that he always works for other people, or that he does only the spectacular and the unusual.

But sometimes he is forced to do the unusual simply because we have gotten so blind to his constancy. Then we do take notice. But if we looked at even this past week, we could see him at work among us: in the peace in our homes, in the health we enjoy, in the happy solution of a problem, in the answer to a prayer, or when we endure the confusion of a crisis—in all those ways our Father walks with us.

Lord, we need the vision to see the Father in his gentle touches. Too often we allow him to be like the Father who tiptoes into the bedroom where a child sleeps to straighten the blankets and kiss him on the forehead. We need to *know* he does that; we need to wake up once in a while to say, "Father, I love you."

Today, Lord, help us to see the loving concern of your Father in our lives and to proclaim his care and his kindness. Today, Lord, is the feast of the Spirit of infinite love!

Part of the Family

Trinity Sunday
Sunday After Pentecost   B

Dt 4:32-34, 39-40
Rom 8:14-17
Mt 28:16-20

The readings of today's Mass should make us pause

whenever we think that the Holy Trinity is merely a doctrine to be believed. The Trinity is more than that. Moses says God is the reality which saves a people from slavery. Paul says that God is a Father adopting us into his family and giving us a whole new spirit of life. Jesus says that in him God is always and forever our companion even to the end of the world. God is our God. He is not only the unapproachable majesty of Sinai. He is also the intimate presence which works for us, frees us and walks with us.

In still other words God has invested himself so heavily in us that in our very act of celebrating him we celebrate ourselves. Not that in ourselves we have much to get excited about. Whenever we are tempted to pat ourselves too hard on the back, we have St. Paul to make us blush: "Name something you have that you have not received. If, then, you have received it, why are you boasting as if it were your own?" (1 Cor 4:7). No, the only way our glorifying ourselves makes sense is to echo the Magnificat.

When we see our greatness in that light, Lord, let us really recognize and proclaim our dignity. Silent tongues in the mouths of children whose Father is King of heaven and earth are a real mystery. They should be crying, "Abba, Father," but too often they are not. And, Lord, until the happiness in our hearts bursts into praise on our tongues, we wonder whether we will ever understand in any depth at all the mystery of the Holy Trinity. The Holy Trinity, Lord, includes us in the family. Never let us forget that magnificent truth.

Sharing the Bread of Angels   Ex 24:3-8
                                  Heb 9:11-15
Corpus Christi   B   Mk 14:12-16, 22-26

We used to sing a fine old Latin hymn entitled "Panis Angelicus" (angelic bread). The words, of course, referred to the Eucharist. But we knew then as we know now that angels eat no bread—they eat nothing; they are pure spirits. So maybe most of us sang the phrases as a poetic play on words that had little reference to any dogmatic reality. And yet it did contain a truth about the Holy Eucharist, one that the second reading emphasizes on today's feast of Christ's Body and Blood.

The author of Hebrews pictures the Lord as entering into the glorious sanctuary of heaven, there to offer an unending Mass in the presence of the Father and of all the angels. He never ceases to give himself in the spiritual sacrifice that brings peace and unity to all creation, and in some way the angels rejoice in the peace created by his death.

And so, of course, do we. Not only is our Mass a remembrance of Christ's historical death and resurrection. We also partake in the unending sacrifice he offers in the timeless "now" of heaven.

Lord Jesus, our Eucharist is an absolutely astounding marriage of the past we call Holy Thursday, Good Friday and Easter Sunday with the eternity we call heaven—an eternity reflected in the present moment of our celebration. Each of us already has one foot in heaven because of you; we already have everlasting life nourished by your Body and Blood. And we have your promise of a final resurrection with you because we have eaten you. Lord, with all the angels of heaven we thank you and praise you.

Awful Indignities 1 Sm 3:3-10, 19
1 Cor 6:13-15, 17-20
2nd Sunday   B Jn 1:35-42

In so many ways the Lord tried to tell us that what he did for us did not just involve the taking away of our sin. Forgiveness of sin was certainly an important part of his work. That is why John the Baptizer calls him the

Lamb of God, the one who turns God's anger away from us by marking our doorposts with his blood.

But the importance of removing our sin is something like the role of the wreckers who come in to destroy an old and unwanted building so that a new structure can go up; it's only a first step. Much more important than making us free of sin was bringing us to share in his risen life by Baptism and the breaking of the bread. Being joined to him as members of his body and as branches of his vine has consequences. When we sin after our Baptism, the sin has a quality it did not have before. After Baptism, we drag the Lord along with us into every act of selfishness. And that ought to horrify us.

It horrified Paul. On the road to Damascus he learned that the Lord identifies completely with all his followers and shares in all their suffering. Paul never forgot. Nor should we. For Paul the sin of being uncharitable is awful not only because it always hurts somebody, but because Christ's body is torn apart by hatred and wrangling. And the sin of unchastity is terrible not only because of its shamefulness, but because it is an affront to the Lord of love under the guise of love.

Lord, you made us to love; you did not make us to lust. You are with us in every act of love, whether it be in the marriage bed or in the giving of a cup of water to the thirsty. But it's also true that you are with us in every act of lust and hatred. You never leave us. Please, Lord, preserve us from subjecting you to awful indignities. Let us love and worship in your Spirit and your truth.

Jonah's Visit　　　　　　　　　Jon 3:1-5, 10
　　　　　　　　　　　　　　　　1 Cor 7:29-31
3rd Sunday   B　　　　　　　　　Mk 1:14-20

There is charm in the story of Jonah in today's first reading—not Jonah's charm but the Ninevites'. In some ways Jonah is very uncharming: He fled the summons to do God's work, and God had almost to sink a ship to bring Jonah to obedience. And then when he succeeded in his mission, he still misread the Lord's mind. He thought that the Lord wanted to destroy a city, but he did not want that at all. He wanted to *save* it. Jonah is a warning to all shepherds, all priests and religious, to do God's work—not just their own.

The Ninevites are great. They were sinners, just like the rest of us. But when the stranger appeared in their streets shouting to them, "Repent; you are sinners, and you must change your ways," they actually listened. And with just a bit of imagination we can appreciate what kind of people they must have been.

Who among us would listen if a man were to walk down the main street of our town tomorrow pointing to each one of us and saying, "You are a sinner. Go to confession *now*"? The image can make us pause. Our cartoonists have made a stock joke out of the bearded and gowned figure carrying a sign announcing the end of the world. We would react with hilarity to the man trying to tell us we are sinners—if we did not punch him first.

None of us likes to be criticized. We find it easy to remember the last person who pointed out our mistake to us—and it takes a very forgiving heart to remember him with a blessing.

Lord, we can really admire the Ninevites. They listened, they respected the messenger and they turned back to you. Would that all of us were as open, kind and generous! Lord, when we need one, send us our Jonah. And when he comes, don't let us kick him out of town!

Our Lord

4th Sunday   B

Dt 18:15-20
1 Cor 7:32-35
Mk 1:21-28

Once in a while we Catholics should try to become aware of what we mean when we say "Our Lord." We use the expression so much that it has practically become Christ's name among us. But when we call him "Lord," we don't always affirm in our hearts what we say with our lips. With our lips we proclaim Christ the Lord and Master of the whole universe won by his death, resurrection and ascension. That was exactly what the first Christians meant when they summed up their whole faith in the rejoicing cry: "Jesus is Lord!" They meant that he rules everything. Everything. And they meant especially that he ruled them. They would not say it until they were readied by the believing community. But when they did finally say it, they pledged themselves to Jesus and to his way. They pledged themselves to follow him, because they saw in him the authority they needed to bring order and peace and joy into their lives.

And what about us? When we call Jesus "Lord" do we proclaim him as the final goal, the final value, the final judge, the final authority on all we say and do and are? Is he really *our* Lord, the Lord of each one of us in those details of life which color our happiness? We can apply a simple-enough test if we really want to. In today's Gospel, the people admired his authority over unclean spirits. Do we allow him to exercise that authority in our own lives?

Lord, you came to conquer every unclean spirit. You showed you had the power to do it, and you shared your power with us. And the uncleanness does not mean just sexual impurity, although that is included. It means every impulse of evil: hatred, cowardice, dishonesty, greed, lackluster worship—all the evils which still fight your Spirit. Drive these unclean spirits from our hearts, Lord. Help each one of us really to mean it when we say: "You are our Lord; you are *my* Lord."

Promise of Happiness　　　　　　　Jb 7:1-4, 6-7
　　　　　　　　　　　　　　　　　　1 Cor 9:16-19, 22-23
5th Sunday　B　　　　　　　　　　　Mk 1:29-39

We often hear that Job was very patient and that he did not complain. But when we hear him in today's first reading, we wonder. He certainly *sounds* as if he were complaining. But maybe complaining and merely philosophizing about the sad human condition are two different things. The only trouble is that when the person who philosophizes is also the person who suffers, the line of distinction gets very thin indeed.

Most of us have known sadness and depression. We know with Job that life on earth is drudgery. We don't feel that way all the time, but when things really get dark and we see no light anywhere, our spirits sink and we wonder whether we will ever feel peace and joy again. Even the fortunate few who rise with song and retire with praise every day certainly know others whose temperaments are not nearly so bouncy. We see around us the widow scrounging for enough money for her family; or the young couple standing beside the burned-out ruins of their new home; or the middle-aged man whose diagnosis of a cancer is a death sentence.

Yes, Lord, Job and we are not strangers. We know sorrow and drudgery, and we complain.

But there is one great difference between him and us—you. Where Job struggled with evil and got very few answers, we see you on the cross and then risen from the dead. We know that we have at least one answer to sorrow and pain and drudgery—they can save us when we bear them with you. With you, Good Friday and Easter Sunday are always linked. Job might think he will not see happiness again. We know we will. You promise it.

Sainthood Now

6th Sunday   B

Lv 13:1-2, 44-46
1 Cor 10:31–11:1
Mk 1:40-45

"Whether you eat or drink—whatever you do—you should do all for the glory of God" (1 Cor 10:31). Advice like that can sometimes discourage us. It can also make us feel very far from a man like Paul. If it was true that Paul followed his own advice and remembered the Lord in everything and at every moment, he had a great gift. We simply do not remember or do all for God's glory. We wish we did, but we don't. We even forget morning and evening prayers. As for remembering the Lord when we work, rest, drive or talk—we usually are too busy with what we are doing to squeeze in other thoughts, even of him.

We wonder if Paul can possibly be speaking to us 20th-century men and women. And the answer comes, as it must: Of course, Paul is speaking to us, and maybe more in this bit of advice than in any other. What Paul asks is not some kind of super-saintliness and unflagging memory characteristic of only a very few Christians. He is speaking of a process we workaday Christians can engage in now and tomorrow and every day.

Lord, teach us a mentality which looks over the day and offers it as a gift. Help us to say, as the 15th-century soldier said on the morning of battle, "Lord, I shall be very busy this day; I may forget thee, but do not thou forget me."

Keep us good today. Anything that is good is yours; the only thing you will not take are evils, sins and selfishness. And let us pray two kinds of prayer: the prayer we say and the prayer we live. And then even our Cokes and burgers will please you!

Am I Faithful? Is 43:1 8-19, 21-22, 24-25
2 Cor 1:18-22
7th Sunday   B Mk 2:1-12

Fidelity is not the most respected word in the English language these days; at least, not respected in practice. It's true that we give a lot of publicity to couples celebrating 50 or more years of marriage, and we are delighted when the man and his wife are still obviously in love with each other. We love, too, to see a veteran priest still joyfully serving his people into his 60's and 70's. And maybe that kind of admiration is our salvation, because we ourselves don't always find fidelity an easy virtue.

Perhaps our difficulty is rooted in the age in which we live. We read of the casual marriages, divorces and living arrangements of famous people. We see television marriages in which bride and groom exchange vows to live together "as long as love shall last." We hear of wife-swapping, and we know of too many cases of marital cheating. And we know how many people have left lives of service so that they can, in today's phrase, find self-fulfillment. Our world is not exactly crowded with examples of heroic fidelity.

It never has been. Fidelity may be helped by the example of others, but, like all other good qualities, it still remains intensely personal. The question for each one of us is, "Am *I* faithful, and will *I* remain faithful to one wife or one husband or to the Church or to anything else that deserves my loyalty?"

When we hear readings like today's, Lord, we would be wise to remember that you call us to be perfect. The Father always makes it possible that we can respond to his call. And you, Lord, are the "yes" which completely fulfills his every promise.

Scripture promises us that perseverance brings salvation. Help us, Lord, to be like you and your Father. Help us to choose a lifetime of good, to promise never to leave it, and then to live it. Help us to be faithful.

In an Age of Change

8th Sunday   B

Hos 2:16-17, 21-22
2 Cor 3:1-6
Mk 2:18-22

Living in any time of change can be very upsetting. We look at our 10- and 11-year-olds, and we can be just a bit envious of the way they have it all together, of the peace and the cheerfulness and the uncluttered state of their lives. But we also know, even if our children don't, that the soon-to-come teen years will shake their peace profoundly. Those years are a time of change: childhood dies and an adult is born. In all deaths and all births suffering must come.

We have seen the same kind of suffering in the world we have known. Those of us who endured World War II knew it as a terrible time of change and upheaval. Perhaps that was why the mood of the 50's was so welcome in at least one way: that decade was comparatively calm and quiet. We had the sense of being between changes. But change came again in the 60's and early 70's. And some of us have been terribly distressed to see alterations in the one institution that we had always thought beyond change: the Roman Catholic Church.

Lord, that distress is a sign of how much we love and need the Church and of how much we love and need you. Never allow any of us who fostered change in the Church to lack respect for those who have suffered because of the change. Those who suffer can teach all of us the necessity of clinging faithfully to what is good.

Lord Jesus, we need so much wisdom to know when old wineskins must be replaced; to know when old structures must be revamped. Dying to the old and welcoming the new is not easy; it is always death and birth, two painful processes. Give us love, understanding and compassion for one another in this, our particular age of change. We need one another. We need you.

In Word and in Deed

9th Sunday   B

Dt 5:12-15
2 Cor 4:6-11
Mk 2:23—3:6

Jesus once shared Isaiah's complaint about people who worship with their lips while their hearts are cold and distant. He also told a tale of two sons asked by their father to work in his fields. One said "yes," but did not go; the other said "no," but then went.

Ultimately, there is no sound evidence of our *being* what the Lord wants except by *doing* his will. We are his friends only if we accept his commands. We can be so fervent in prayer, so joyous at Mass. We can be great teachers and preachers of his Word. But if our fervor and eloquence are not rooted in our willingness to do his will, we are what St. Paul describes: a noisy gong, a clanging cymbal.

All this must be in Paul's mind when he tells us that we are to reflect to the world God's own light shining in our hearts. But he reminds us that we keep God's great gift in vessels of fragile clay. The Spirit given to us in Baptism comes into weak, unstable human beings. Paul warns us to expect affliction and persecution; the Spirit offers no guarantee against suffering. It is because we can offer praise from sorrowing hearts that we are living signs of God's presence.

Lord, let our words and emotions support our acts, but never let us try to use them as substitutes. We cannot talk our way into your kingdom. We know that suffering and words are sometimes very distant relatives. If we are moved to tears before *your* cross and moved to flee from *our* cross, we are still far from you. Lord, let our prayer and our life be one.

Open to Goodness

10th Sunday   B

Gn 3:9-15
2 Cor 4:13–5:1
Mk 3:20-35

"I give you my word, every sin will be forgiven mankind and all the blasphemies men utter, but whoever blasphemes against the Holy Spirit will never be forgiven" (Mk 3:28-29a). We like the first part of that sentence. We know we sin, and we count on infinite forgiveness; we know the Lord will welcome us back at least the 70 times seven times he demanded from Peter. But the rest can confuse us. Is the Lord's willingness to forgive not limitless after all? Is there a sin which is greater than his love?

Even the questions can stagger us. We see such evils in the world: murder, adultery, fraud and thievery. We count millions of abortions; we remember Dachau. All of these can be forgiven, and the sin against the Holy Spirit cannot? What *is* this horrible sin? What in heaven's name can finally turn the Lord away from us?

The answer is also in today's Gospel. It is in the accusation brought against Jesus by the examiners sent from Jerusalem to interpret officially the source of his power. Their final judgment was that he was possessed. His cures and his miracles, his teachings and his kindness—all those ways by which he revealed the Father's love—the inquisitors say came from the devil. Evil, say the scribes, produces all this good. But that is wrong, a perverse and a foolish judgment. If the scribes persist in their judgment, they will never learn where true good is. They will never accept the Lord. They will never see the real God. They are lost forever.

The sin against the Holy Spirit, Lord, is what you plainly showed it to be: a sin of hardhearted bad judgment. And we can still commit it every time we judge somebody's goodness as the product of evil intention: "Oh yes, he gave a lot of money, but all he wants is praise."

Lord, keep us away from that kind of thinking.

Keep us open to goodness. Keep us kind in our reaction. Keep us like you.

Trusting Farmers Ez 17:22-24
2 Cor 5:6-10
11th Sunday   B Mk 4:26-34

People who have green thumbs know the pleasure of planting a row of seeds in the ground, watching the tiny sprouts push out of the earth, and then doing just what is needed to nurture the plant to fruitfulness. And sometimes just letting the plant alone is as necessary as a lot of fussing.

We know the story about the foolish farmer who used to dig up the plants to see how the roots were doing. But we whose thumbs are any color but green do some equally silly things. We imagine that *we* have to *make* the plants grow; we forget that our job is simply to set up the right conditions. The plant will then grow by itself.

And so will the Church. Today's Gospel tells us that the kingdom of heaven is like a seed planted in the earth and developing quite adequately even while the farmer sleeps. It warns us against a feverish concern that the work of the Church depends completely on our intelligence or our zeal, our organizational strength, our managerial expertise, or our fiscal responsibility. All these things may and do enter into our parochial life. But they do not make or break the Church. They are only conditions surrounding the real life of the Church. And the real life of the Church is participation in the divine life of the Trinity.

This life, Lord, goes on by its own laws and at its own speed in the lives of each one of us. Some of us may be gifted with it more abundantly than others. Some certainly respond to it more generously than others. But the important thing each one of us must recognize is that you are always the giver, and what

you give is complete life.

Our job is to receive your life with joy, thanks and praise, to cooperate and to be happy in our privileges. Echoing Paul's confidence in today's second reading, we ask again and again for the joy of your salvation. Keep us from the foolish anxiety of the farmer who does not trust the plant to do its job.

Call to Trust Jb 38:1, 8-11
2 Cor 5:14-17
12th Sunday   B Mk 4:35-41

The Gospels offer some astonishing stories: the raising to life of the widow's son at Naim, the curing of the blind, the deaf, the lame and the leprous; huge crowds fed with a few pieces of fish and a few loaves of bread. We sometimes wonder why our eyes are not popping out of our heads as we read these stories. Have we heard them so often that all their wonder is gone?

The story in today's Gospel is a case in point. Why doesn't the stilling of the storm stagger us? Certainly the apostles wondered—and so, for them, part of the reason for working the wonder is fulfilled. They see in Jesus something they had not suspected: a power greater than wind and sea.

But the other reason for the miracle was perhaps not so successful. In a very real sense, Christ would have been happier not to have had to calm the waves. He would much rather have had the apostles place their trust in his presence. But they did not have that kind of trust, and so they panicked. At least, though, they turned to him in that panic. And he took care of them. But he also rebuked them for their lack of faith.

Lord, you asked an awful lot of your apostles. But it is also true that if they had been able to give the trust you asked, they would have been so much happier and full of peace.

And so it is with us, Lord. We cry out to you from all our trouble and pain, from illness and tragedy and agony. You scold us for our lack of faith. You invite us to trust you, to rest secure in your power to save us.

Lord, give us this kind of faith. Help us to trust no matter what happens, even in the face of death.

Relying on the Lord Wis 1:13-15; 2:23-24
2 Cor 8:7, 9, 13-15
13th Sunday B Mk 5:21-43

If any sentence reveals to us the true nature of our relationship to the Lord, it is this sentence in today's Gospel: "Fear is useless. What is needed is trust" (Mk 5:36b). If only we could take that advice into the depths of our hearts and really rejoice in it and live by it!

Fear is useless, says the Lord. How do we trust beyond our fear? It happens often enough in our lives. We fear an operation, and yet we trust the surgeon; we fear an airplane trip, and yet we trust the pilot.

Perhaps the only thing we need fear is ourselves. We fearfully wonder if we will accept God's help, allow him to be our Father. Will we try to love our neighbor as ourselves? But the interesting thing about that kind of fear is that it immediately makes us cry, "Help! I can't do it alone, Lord. Come to my assistance."

Our fear about ourselves can lead us to greater reliance on the Lord. For if anything should be clear to us, it is that we need never fear that he will ignore us. Fear about his power and love is foolish.

Lord, what is needed in each one of us is trust. Do we need a better job? Let us trust you. Have we troubles with our children? Let us trust you. Have we just received a diagnosis of cancer? Let us trust you. No matter what onslaught the evil spirit has launched against us, its power still does not equal yours.

Yours is always the ultimate victory, either on this

side of the grave or on the other. Only you conquered death. Only you can bring us through every dark valley, Lord. Help us to trust that your goodness and kindness will follow us all the days of our lives—and beyond.

A Prophet in His Own Country

Ez 2:2-5
2 Cor 12:7-10
Mk 6:1-6

14th Sunday B

We have made a stock comic figure out of the person who covers his ears and says: "I don't want to hear about it!" And maybe the figure is comic because we see a lot of ourselves in it.

Some of us have an acutely developed ability to hear only what we want to hear. Sometimes we want to hear only the flattering things about ourselves—and so we become conveniently deaf when someone tells us, "Maybe you could do the job better another way." Or perhaps we cannot bear to think that our children are less than perfect—and so we blame every failure of theirs on their teachers or classmates or friends. In effect, this means we implicitly say, "I don't see how I can have anything but the truth, and nobody can tell me otherwise." If we were wiser, we would have the humility to add: "Don't confuse me with the facts."

The prophets had a hard time because they had to speak to people whose minds were closed to what God's messengers had to say. In the first reading Ezekiel is warned that he might not be welcomed with enthusiasm by the people; and most certainly he was not. Most prophets were not.

The Lord himself spoke of the blood of the prophets that had been shed in Israel's long history. And in today's Gospel he collides with the closed mentality of his own townspeople, a mentality which registered amazement at his deeds and words, but then rejected him because he did not fit into its preconceived pattern. He was only one of them—too familiar, too ordinary to be recognized as anyone special.

     Lord Jesus, save us from that mentality. Save us from the poison of prejudice that categorizes without thinking. Save us from turning a person off because he says a truth we would rather not hear. Protect us from the arrogance of the Pharisees who could tell the blind man he was born in sin and had no right to teach them.
     Lord, you came in a way your townspeople could not accept, and you come to us in ways that we do not always expect. You come in all types of persons, especially the poor and the hungry, and that can confuse us because we always expect to see you as God. When you come, don't let us be blind or deaf to you, however unexpectedly you appear. We don't want to miss you!

The Call to Apostleship Am 7:12-15
Eph 1:3-14
15th Sunday B Mk 6:7-13

     The Lord does a momentous thing in today's Gospel. Only six chapters deep into this book, Mark has him sending his apostles out to participate in his fight against sin in all of its evil shapes.
     Jesus had prepared them for their work when he selected them at the start of his ministry. He never wanted these men to be only disciples, people sitting at his feet to listen. He wanted them to add apostleship to their discipleship. He wanted them, after they had heard him, to go and bring him to others.
     And that is momentous, truly momentous. The Lord asks human beings to do his work, not because he was to become some kind of business manager, but because he knew that he too was human and was going to die. A time would come when Jesus would no longer be with his followers in the way they had known. His followers would then have to take over. But what a responsibility! A privilege, yes, but also a heavy burden.

The Lord saved the world, but he is God-made-man. He asks mere human beings to carry that salvation of his to those he was not able to meet. He must have trusted them to do what he expected, but he also gave them a portion of his empowering Spirit. In that strength they went forth, and the Lord was with them even through the cruel deaths many had to die.

Lord, what about us? You first sent fishermen and a tax-collector out on that early mission. We are certainly not lower on the social scale than they were. Many of us are college-trained. Many of us have responsible jobs. Most of us are respected. Do you expect us to pass beyond discipleship into apostleship too? You must, for we have been confirmed in the Spirit. Of course you want us to be apostles. Lord, help us then to bear your burden. Help us to be *you* to those we meet.

Shepherds and Sheep Jer 23:1-6
Eph 2:13-18
16th Sunday   B Mk 6:30-34

These readings today make us think about our own shepherds, particularly our priests. Jeremiah is harsh in the words he speaks concerning priests and kings, the shepherds of his time. We wonder whether some of those same warnings could not be directed against our own priests. Certainly, men ordained for service who now know nothing but how to dominate and frighten are not priests after the Lord's heart. Certainly, those priests whose hands are always out for money and who grow fat and sleek at the parishioners' expense are men the Father might condemn. Certainly, those priests who seek advancement up the ecclesiastical ladder rather than the will of God will perish while preaching to others.

Our priests today stand under the mandate given to the apostles: to serve, really serve, the sheep. Any mandate they assume on their own is a temptation and a diversion.

But it is also true that our priests need the support of the parishioners. Many a priestly life has been made bitter and unhappy because parishioners have refused to cooperate, have been unkind, have carped and criticized and tried to undermine every priestly initiative. Some priests who have tried to follow extremely popular predecessors could get little help from the parishioners. These priests had the misfortune of being different persons; but how could they have been anything else?

Lord, if you have harsh words against unworthy priests, you have equally strong judgments for bitter-spirited parishioners. Sheep and shepherd need each other. Give our priests a true pastoral sense. Give us openness, kindness and helpfulness. Help us to work together in your love.

Keeping the Peace 2 Kgs 4:42-44
Eph 4:1-6
17th Sunday   B Jn 6:1-15

Peace was the Lord's last gift to his friends. Like all the rest of his saving work, the peace we have in our hearts and in our congregation is his gift to us, freely given and never withdrawn. Then why are we so often uneasy in our hearts and at odds with one another in our relationships? Why are we so dissatisfied with the conditions of our daily life that we crave a past that will never return or a future that might not ever come?

Perhaps we have no peace because we have not yet learned how to accept a gift. We seem sometimes unable to see how completely unearned a gift always is. Maybe our early experiences as children at Christmas have conditioned us to expect gifts only when we have been "good little boys and girls." We forget that the Lord's

gifts to us don't follow that kind of pattern at all. He
loved us when we were still sinners, and he continues
to love us even when we don't stop sinning.

Despite all that, we still try to make everything
depend on *us*. We often lack peace because we are so
concerned about how far *we* still have to go.

**Of course we do have far to go, Lord, but we ought
always to remember that without you we will never get
there. We too often ignore the gift we already have: the
Spirit, who is always in our hearts, calling us to unity
and peace.**

**Lord, you and your Spirit are already our peace. If
we acknowledge that reality, we then go forward in love
and joy to *keep* the peace. Lord, help us!**

Abandoning Illusions

18th Sunday   B

Ex 16:2-4, 12-15
Eph 4:17, 20-24
Jn 6:24-35

No wonder the Lord chose Paul to be one of his
first preachers. The man was a genius. That's not to say
that God doesn't sometimes work with unfit instruments. But he saw in Paul a man of subtle mind and
deep awareness of what makes people tick. He used him,
and we are the gainers. For example, in today's second
reading, Paul tells the Ephesians to abandon their "former way of life and the old self which deteriorates
through illusion and desire" (Eph 4:22). And we hear
the wisdom in his words.

Illusion *can* cause us to decay. We love to clutch
our illusions and dignify them by the name of "hope,"
but a great abyss separates the two. Hope, real hope,
rests on conviction. We hope for heaven. We know it
will be ours; and our hope is firm, because it rests on
the Lord's promise to prepare a place for us. On another
level, we go to an airport in the hope of seeing a friend
arrive. The hope is firm, because we have a telegram

saying he is coming.

But illusions are very different from hope. We can sometimes have the illusion that we will go to heaven even though we completely ignore the Lord's commands. Illusion would send us to the airport to wait for a friend who has never said he will come.

Lord, if all our life is lived in illusions, in vain hopes and foolish pursuits, we are in a sad state of decay. We can so easily delude ourselves every time we forget that you alone are the way, the truth and the life. Make us be sensible, Lord. Make all our hope rest in you. Then indeed we will never be disappointed.

A Loving Family

19th Sunday   B

1 Kgs 19:4-8
Eph 4:30—5:2
Jn 6:41-51

Sometimes we have the great privilege of sitting in the living room of a family whose love and respect for one another is almost tangible. We see the happy pride in the eyes of the parents as they talk with the children or as they say goodnight to a teenager off on a date. And perhaps even more impressive is the quiet affection the children show each other, even in their teasing. Homes like these are evidence that Paul was right to compare the love of husband and wife to the Lord's love for his Church. The love between a man and a woman is absorbed and reflected by their children. In a very real sense the happy home is a little Church.

But what about the big Church—the congregation to which we belong? Have we some of the qualities of the little Church, the family? Are we proud of one another and joyful in the happiness of everyone else? Do we help and affirm each other in the good qualities we all so obviously have? And do we sympathize with the ones who suffer? These characteristics are so homey, so familial, and so easy to show.

What do we lose by a smile and a handshake when we come together to pray? Nothing—except a bit of our icy reserve. And what do we gain by introducing into the congregation some of the same fracturing qualities that disturb homes: criticism, aggressive anger, constant bickering, judging and downgrading each other? Nothing—except a bitter satisfaction that shrivels our hearts and weakens us all in our search for peace.

Lord, Paul tells us today not to sadden the Holy Spirit. We would be a happy congregation if we were sensitive to the Spirit of peaceful unity. Bitterness, passion and anger, harsh words, slander and malice divide us. What homes and parishes we would have if we erased all these things! Help each one of us to say, "It must start with me. I can't wait for anyone else."

Forsaking Foolishness

20th Sunday   B

Prv 9:1-6
Eph 5:15-20
Jn 6:51-58

Often we have warned ourselves about being foolish. Today's readings invite us to reflect a bit more deeply on our lack of wisdom. The first reading tells us to forsake foolishness so that we might live; Paul tells us not to act like fools; and the Lord is implicitly urging his hearers in today's Gospel not to be so foolish as to reject him when he offers his body and blood as their food. In rejecting him they reject their own everlasting life.

Such foolishness is sometimes present in our lives—perhaps more so in our everyday lives than in the obviously big decisions that shape our futures. At those decisive junctures we usually think, weigh consequences and sift motives. But even at those crossroads we can be foolish. Choosing somebody to marry is a decision that colors every other decision for the rest of our days, but hasty marriages have certainly given many people leisure to repent. And any sensible person would say that a job can be a source of deep satisfaction or of grating frustration—and yet it's amazing how many of us just tumble into the jobs we have. Even in great matters we don't always use our heads.

But it is in the everyday routine that we can find pervasive foolishness, and nowhere more so than in a day without prayer.

You know, Lord, how frequent those days can be. We rise, we eat, we work and come home, we watch TV and go to bed. And our thoughts of any reality other than the immediate are rare. Maybe, Lord, this is the greatest foolishness of all. It is the folly of living without you. It is the stupidity of never turning to freshness and new life, love and strength. How much more foolish can we get?

Lord, you are always found in the present moment. We will never find you in the past; nor is our strength renewed by thinking we will pray tomorrow. You are the eternal now. Help us, Lord, to turn to you in the now of our life, for this way is wise. Help us to stop being fools.

Responsive Love   Jos 24:1-2, 15-17, 18
                                                  Eph 5:21-32

21st Sunday   B   Jn 6:60-69

It is a shame that so many want to rip out the passage from Paul's Letter to the Ephesians that was read at Mass today. The trouble, of course, is with the word *submissive*. It smacks of slavery and bondage. Many women today have no desire to be submissive to anyone, including a husband. They will love him, cooperate with him, talk with him, work with him—but they will not put themselves into a state of constant deference to him. They reserve the right to disagree, and they want the responsibility of joining in family decision-making.

But Paul is not so far from those desires. He just approaches a cooperative marital union more from the viewpoint of the husband. He tells husbands to love their wives. How much? ". . .[A]s they do their own bodies" (Eph 5:28a). If all husbands responded as sensitively and quickly to their wives' needs as they do to the needs of their own bodies, we would have no divorces or separations or philanderings.

Just think of it. A husband is hungry—and gets himself a sandwich. A wife is depressed—and her husband senses her mood as accurately as he senses his own hunger. He immediately does what he can to cheer her, for after all, he loves her as he loves his own body.

Lord, men with that kind of sensitivity are the joy of their wives for the simple reason that to love another as one loves oneself is the fulfillment of the Law. And the submission Paul asks of wives is the same: to be as responsive to her husband as the Church is to you. That Lord, is complete responsiveness. It is the human openness to God that we call faith. Responsiveness is much more than mere submission, just as faith is much more than fear.

Lord, love is always a two-way street. Unrequited love is tragic in marriage. Love is made to be given and received. Lord, make us into sensitive, responsive husbands and wives!

Order Out of Chaos

22nd Sunday   B

Dt 4:1-2, 6-8
Jas 1:17-18, 21-22, 27
Mk 7:1-8, 14-15, 21-23

It is interesting to see how uncomfortable we can become when we have too many alternatives to pick from, too many decisions to make. Our first impulse is to try to simplify things, to reduce them to some kind of system. The effort is made by a mother trying to get four children off to school or an office-manager trying to channel an inundation of paper. The mother almost instinctively tries to get some kind of system established, if for no other reason than to maintain her own sanity. And people make a living in business by channeling data to proper offices in the organization. We can live with chaos just so long; after that, most of us say, "Enough!" and work towards some kind of order.

Maybe that impulse was at work in the Lord when he scolded the religious leaders of his time for disregarding God's commandment and clinging to human tradition. By Jesus' time the people of Israel did not have 10 commandments to follow; the 10 had mushroomed to 613. By our time they have ballooned even further. All we need to do to be frightened by the complexity of our legal system is to read the instructions on our income-tax form each year—or try to.

Lord, you tried to bring some order into the legal chaos of your day. You simplified all the commandments to two: loving God and loving neighbor. Perversely, though, we have multiplied laws again and again. It's time for us once more to say, "Enough!"—to separate God's commandment from human tradition.

Lord, help us to be like you. Help us always to keep first things first. Help us to learn that law without love is chaos.

Call to Openness   Is 35:4-7
                     Jas 2:1-5
23rd Sunday B   Mk 7:31-37

The deaf and dumb have not disappeared from among us. We still need the Lord's touch to heal our afflictions. Not only do we need him to cure us of our inability to hear or speak physical sounds; we also need his help to hear and report on his coming to each of us. For he does communicate with us. No day of our life passes without his touching us in some way. But we are often closed to him, and we are not sure how to open our ears.

The religious leaders of Christ's time thought they had God completely figured out. When Jesus came, he was a puzzle to them, and, they thought, a danger. So they killed him—hardly a very satisfactory solution. We still think we know all the ways the Spirit works. We can miss him when he comes in unfamiliar patterns—like renewed emphasis on Scripture or congregational participation in worship. We can miss him in sickness or joy, in friendship, beauty or kindness.

Lord, none of us is ever completely open to you. In the center of each heart stands a wall against you. When we are closed and stingy, when we are absolutely sure we have every one of your moves figured out, then you cannot surprise us with your love. Then we need openness, then we are deaf and dumb. We cannot hear you come, and so we cannot announce your presence to others who need you.

Lord, let us hear your call to openness. Surprise us with all your loving ingenuity.

A Different Kind of Love

24th Sunday   B

Is 50:4-9
Jas 2:14-18
Mk 8:27-35

Is it possible that we today could still be trying to change the Lord's mind about the best way to do things? Peter, in today's Gospel, tried to tell Jesus that he could not possibly be right about how his life would end; and Christ's reply to him was very sharp indeed: "Get out of my sight, you satan! You are not judging by God's standards but by man's!" (Mk 8:33).

What a frightening thing to hear! We, with the benefit of 2,000 years of hindsight, know that Jesus was right and Peter was very wrong. Yet Peter spoke out of love. Apparently love is not enough. Or maybe our ways of loving are not always God's ways.

Our love always tries to exclude suffering. We don't like suffering, either for ourselves or for those we love. And that's not to say that Jesus did like suffering, but that he approached it differently than we do. To him, it was not something to be avoided at all costs, but the ultimate proof that his love was real, his faithfulness enduring, his concern for us greater than his fear of death.

Lord, sometimes we show that kind of love, too. We read of policemen and firemen dying so that others might be saved; we hear of parents depriving themselves so that their children can have advantages. We hear of children heroically bearing the burdens of cruel and alcoholic parents. We do indeed know that suffering is sometimes the only road to great good. But we don't like the path.

And so we try so hard to be sure that we will never suffer. It's a vain attempt, Lord. Teach us that. Teach us that pain comes with birth and living and dying. Teach us to make each pain part of your redemptive Calvary.

Welcoming the Little Ones — Wis 2:17-20

Jas 3:16—4:3

25th Sunday B — Mk 9:30-37

One of the greatest things we see in church each Sunday is the number of young families coming to Mass together. They come up to receive Communion: the father carrying a little one in his arms, the mother tugging another little one by the hand. Sometimes the children watch wide-eyed as the parents receive. Scenes like these are exactly what the Lord speaks of in today's Gospel.

Jesus takes a little child from the crowd, puts his arms around him, and invites his listeners to welcome him in the innocent. He sets a priority for us. He tells us that these little children are among the most precious realities in our lives. They are precious because they embody our own love for one another. A husband and wife see one another in the eyes of their child. And they are precious because in the child Jesus enters the home in a special kind of way.

If we take Jesus seriously, we must see our children as unique expressions of the sacramental grace he promises when we marry. For "sacramental grace" is simply the name we give to his constant daily presence in our marriages, a presence we give to one another as surely as the priest brings his presence to us in bread and wine.

Lord, we give the sacrament of matrimony to each other. We give *you* to each other. And when we hear your words to us today inviting us to welcome children into our midst for your sake, we look at our own children. We gather them in our arms, we kiss them and we bless you for making something so easy and so natural also a great act of love of you.

Lord, help us to expand our hearts more and more in a deep and loving service of our own children. Help us, too, to love and help all children. When we see them may we see you—and your Father in you.

Faithful to His Spirit

Nm 11:25-29
Jas 5:1-6
Mk 9:38-43, 45, 47-48

26th Sunday   B

Moses must have been a wonderful man. He was Hebrew-born but raised as an Egyptian and could have spent his life as a court favorite. Yet he chose to cast his lot with his own people, and so had to go into exile.

When God tapped him for service, he did not glory in the power offered him. Humility was the essence of his being. Possessing overwhelming evidence of the Father's favor towards him, knowing what a wonderful gift that favor was, he did not grasp it jealously. He wanted to share God's love, and was positively pleased to see others receive the spirit of God. Moses was a humble, generous, loving man.

And so, of course, was Jesus. It was characteristic of him to want others to share his ministry and his power from the earliest days of his public life. One of the first things he did was to choose his co-workers. So when we hear him affirm that those who are not against us are our companions on his way, it should not surprise us. We ought to be really pleased.

Lord, you open so many opportunities for friendship to us. You invite us to cooperate with those who, although not one of us, seek your way. We see so many loving and generous people in this world who are not Catholic or even Christian. They are one with us in their thirst for justice and their efforts to do good.

Lord, like you, may we welcome and treasure the people who travel other roads than ours toward you. Pour out your Spirit upon them.

Made in Heaven Gn 2:18-24
Hb 2:9-11
27th Sunday   B Mk 10:2-16

Marriages, according to the old saying, are made in heaven. Years of experience and testing uncovered the truth contained in those words. Experience has also added a corollary proverb: Marriages might have been made in heaven, but they are lived on earth.

Marriages were indeed made in heaven. The Father wanted man and woman to live together as husband and wife, because the two needed each other so much. The author of the Genesis story expresses it vividly. He portrays man and woman as originally one person, striving in marriage to become again one flesh. If anything shows how essential is the need of man and woman for each other, that story does. It enables us to see the plan of God: We are to complete each other as persons.

But marriages are also lived on earth. Each of us must search for the right partner among the thousands of people we meet. And when we finally choose, we choose not only *for* someone, but also *against* all others. Both of those choices can cause us problems; we are human and fully fallible.

> Guide us, Lord, in the search. Help us to know each other well before marriage; preserve us from making foolish mistakes. Help us, too, to remember that we choose against every other possible partner. When someone new excites us, help us not to be surprised, for we are still human. Help us just to make the right choice— to affirm our first choice. Keep us off the dead-end street of adultery.

Beyond the Law　　　　　　　　Wis 7:7-11
　　　　　　　　　　　　　　　　Heb 4:12-13
28th Sunday　B　　　　　　　　Mk 10:17-30

The young man in today's Gospel is no stranger to us if we look seriously at our experience and our relationships. We know by now that the commandments are inadequate to control the direction of our lives. They are important, certainly, but they are not sufficient to guide us in the best and most important moments of life.

The law forbids the taking of life. We are not inclined to murder. We are sickened by stories of war and violence in the daily newspaper. We deplore the legalization of abortion and speak for the rights of the unborn. But to refrain from killing is only half a value. To love and cherish life is the other half; and the ways in which we do that are not covered by the commandment.

The Lord asks us to go beyond the law, to love as

he loved. That means sitting up all night with a sick child, campaigning for adequate housing for the elderly, gathering food for the hungry—however the Lord calls us to love and cherish the life he has given. For we are made in the image and likeness of the Father. Our great mission is to allow that image to develop in all people, and to fight anything that degrades it. Commandments are necessary, but they are not enough.

Lord, we need the urging of your Spirit to lead us into creative respect for life. Let us not only preserve life, but cherish it and help it flourish. Then your likeness will be seen in us.

Refined in the Awful Mill   Is 53:10-11
                                Heb 4:14-16
29th Sunday   B   Mk 10:35-45

All of us can smile at the cartoon character who doesn't want any downs in life, only ups, ups, ups! That character speaks to us—if we had our way, our life would be a staircase of ascending happiness and we would never have a toothache. But, of course, we don't have our way. Our life is not unalloyed joy, and we do have aches and pains. We have the lifelong job of learning the hardest of all lessons: to accept life as it really is and to stop constructing plans that will remove every cross from our path.

Scripture describes the generosity with which Jesus accepted the cross. The prophet Isaiah saw the power that resided in the person willing to accept suffering. In today's first reading he sets before us the figure of God's suffering servant.

The good that comes from suffering will never be easy to explain. But good does come; that is a fact. Through suffering, the Lord won a world. We all know remarkable people who seemed to be refined in the awful mill of suffering until only gentleness, kindness and beauty remain. We know old people in nursing homes whom life has deprived of everything except a loving and generous heart. Their smiles are light to the world. We have seen youngsters who have known nothing but pain and crutches all their lives; and their bright spirits strengthen us all.

Lord, suffering hurts; suffering is awful. But it can and does help us grow. When Calvary looms before us, help us through Gethsemane; keep Easter before our eyes. We need you to walk with us.

Discovering Our Blind Spots

Jer 31:7-9
Heb 5:1-6
Mk 10:46-52

30th Sunday   B

Physical blindness has at least one advantage: It is recognizable. A person without sight knows he is blind and learns to compensate as best he can. Other people know he is blind and offer help.

But there is a form of blindness that is not so evident. We use the expression "blind spot" to describe it. A blind spot is an inability to judge accurately the reality of a situation. A person whose lack of organizational skills makes him a poor manager can be blind to the real creative abilities he possesses. A blind spot about blacks can lead a person to see every report about black crime as an indictment of an entire race, and every black advantage as a concession to "those people." A husband and wife may develop a blind spot to the necessity of expressing their love on special occasions.

Blind spots are, in their own way, as dangerous as physical blindness. Perhaps even more so, for those who suffer them are unaware of their own blindness, and never ask for help. But if we have a blind spot, we are indeed in need of healing. We see only part of the human landscape, and what we do not see we judge according to deeply imbedded patterns that are hard to change. We protest our love to a spouse who is hurt by a forgotten anniversary. Or we acclaim a heroic black for "acting white."

Lord, help us to discover our blind spots. Let us see them as dangerous stumbling blocks in our commitment to love and justice. Help us to recognize our prejudices. Lord, today we pray for sight!

Wholehearted Love Dt 6:2-6
Heb 7:23-28
31st Sunday   B Mk 12:28-34

Today is the beginning of the Church year's end. The feast of Christ the King is only three Sundays away. It is time to sift out the important realities over which we have prayed each Sunday all year long.

The Church offers for our reflection the very core of our relationship with God: love. Not just a bubbly, emotional, up-and-down kind of love, but love that seizes us in the deepest part of our being, colors all our thoughts and decisions, and gives strength and vitality to our daily life. We are commanded to love God with our heart, our soul, our strength. He will not be satisfied with mere words that spring from the lips without involving the heart. He wants something much more: a love that reflects his love for us. He wants a *whole* love from us. That should not surprise us; we want the same kind of love from one another.

We know how easily we can fool ourselves on this question of love. We have manhandled the word almost beyond recognition. A TV commercial once suggested that love is like ginger ale—bubbly, sparkling and light. But love is really more like blood—the very essence of life. And like life, it is of one piece. To profess love of God and hate one's neighbor is impossible; it is to take the stance of a liar (1 Jn 4:20).

Lord, fill our hearts with love. Let us live our love for you in love for one another. Forgive our hesitant hearts and fill them with your love, your life, your joy.

Open Our Hearts

32nd Sunday   B

1 Kgs 17:10-16
Heb 9:24-28
Mk 12:38-44

We continue to pray and reflect on love. Today's readings focus on one aspect of love—generosity. Not just generosity off the top of the bankroll, but generosity that carries the mark of wholehearted love.

To illustrate that the Lord measures the size of a gift by the size of the giving heart, the Gospel tells the story of the widow's offering. Her few pennies represent all she has. She held nothing back, but gave with all her heart. This is complete generosity.

The widow who welcomes Elijah is just as prodigal. She seems even poorer than the widow at the temple: All this widow has is a little oil and flour. We have to use our imagination to realize the leap of faith she made when she heeded Elijah's request. If our bishop asked us to withdraw all our savings and give them to the Church, we would recoil in fear. But Elijah's widow did not. She depended on the care of the Lord, while we continue to struggle and worry for our future. Which is the wiser?

Lord, you would not strip us of security. You never ask more than we have to give. The one thing you ask is that our hearts be generous, loving and open to your suggestions. For our generosity to others opens our hearts to the abundance of your gifts, and you will never be outdone in generosity. Lord, open our hearts!

All in All

33rd Sunday   B

Dn 12:1-3
Heb 10:11-14, 18
Mk 13:24-32

Today we are urged to lift our eyes beyond the cares of the present moment and to see the one who is the boundary of our existence. Beyond the horizons of today we can glimpse the final triumph of Jesus Christ.

Already we have been swept up into his final victory. He has joined us to himself in Baptism and given us a share in his Easter triumph. He walks with us every day of our lives, encouraging us to let him be all in all for us. He waits for us when we wander from his path, and opens his arms in welcome on our return.

Sin and death are defeated. Sickness and loneliness, pain and separation will mar creation no more on the day of the Lord's return. Even now, they cannot overcome us. The Lord will never allow us to be tempted beyond our strength. The bright Easter morning dawns beyond every Calvary.

Lord Jesus, you are the Alpha and the Omega. You are the beginning and the end. You are the Word once spoken to bring all things into being. In you, all persons, all things, all times will be gathered together in a perfect song of praise to the Father. You, Lord Jesus, are all in all.

Testifying to the Truth

34th or Last Sunday of the Year
Christ the King   B

Dn 7:13-14
Rv 1:5-8
Jn 18:33-37

This last Sunday sums up the message of the entire Church year. Very simply, it has been about the coming of the Father's kingdom onto this earth. For Americans inexperienced with the royal form of government, the correction Jesus gives to Pilate is particularly apt. When

Pilate questions Jesus about his kingdom, he replies that his mission is rather to testify to the truth.

If we Americans have trouble with the feast of Christ the King, we can hardly say that we have trouble with Christ's coming to testify to the truth.

There is something absolutely noble about a person who testifies to the truth when everybody else is captivated by a lie. It is certainly no way to become popular. We think of Jeremiah telling his countrymen: "Do not fight the invaders. They are Yahweh's punishment for us." For his testimony he was thrown into a watery pit. We think of John the Baptizer telling Herod he has committed incest. John was killed. Or we think of those rare people who rise in a public meeting to ask for charity and justice when everybody else in the room wants only a perpetuation of prejudice. Life is not easy for those who testify to the truth.

Lord, you led the way in that most difficult of all missions. You spoke the truth to religious leaders who did not want their established power shaken. You spoke to ordinary people, some of whom said yes to you—and others who walked away. And you spoke to Pilate, the sophisticated Roman, whose only response to you was the weary, "Truth. . . . What does that mean?" (Jn 18: 38a). Lord, you testified; you did not refuse to witness to the truth. You, and others like you, are our real nobility. You are our real king. Help us to share your courage and integrity.

Cycle C

Discovering a Fresh Creation

1st Sunday of Advent   C

Jer 33:14-16
1 Thes 3:12—4:2
Lk 21:25-28, 34-36

Once again we give thanks for a fresh start, a new year in which to allow the Lord to become the most important person in our lives.

If we could dig deeply enough into ourselves and into the reality that surrounds us, we would find inexhaustible freshness. But we live too much on the surface of our lives, a surface that we soil and scar by our selfishness.

Our problem is that we have lost sight of the Father's image within us. We have allowed our spirits to "become bloated with indulgence and drunkenness and worldly cares" (Lk 21:34). We have lived a full year since the first Sunday of last Advent, and we are not completely proud of our record. No matter. Today we begin again.

Lord, deepen our vision to see the freshness within all things. This is the quality everything incessantly receives from the creating hand of your Father; and he is never stale, never wearying, never repetitive. Help us to see in each other a glorious creation, unique and lovely, impressed with the Father's image.

Lord, make us overflow with love. Our own deep-down freshness is straining to be released. Our gift of your Spirit has lain unused and neglected too long. Refresh us, Lord, renew us and cleanse us for your coming. Light up the Christmas already in our hearts!

Celebrating His Coming

2nd Sunday of Advent   C

Bar 5:1-9
Phil 1:4-6, 8-11
Lk 3:1-6

Paul offers an important Advent truth in the second reading today: "He who has begun the good work in you will carry it through to completion, right up to the day of Christ Jesus" (Phil 1:6). We need to be reminded that indeed the good work has begun in us. It began when we were united to Christ in Baptism and Confirmation by the gift of the Spirit.

We sometimes play a little game during Advent, pretending to ourselves and especially to our children that we are preparing to welcome the Lord into our world. But that really *is* a game, and perhaps a dangerous one. For Advent is not a time of waiting for him to come; Advent is a time of preparing to *celebrate* his coming.

There is a world of difference between the two attitudes. If we pretend for these four weeks that Jesus is merely on his way, we deny his constant presence among us. But if we prepare ourselves for four weeks to celebrate his presence, we say yes to two truths: that he has begun a great work in us for which we offer thanks and praise; and that this work is not finished, a task for which we need his help and our own effort.

This is what Paul is emphasizing when he prays that we hold fast to essential values. In other words we need to value the work the Lord has begun in us. And these four weeks of Advent are splendid days to become more aware of his gift, more appreciative and more sensitive to how we have used it.

Lord, our conscience is not clear. The tensions of the past year have often sapped our desire to be open to you and kind to our family and our friends. In this season, cleanse our conscience. Awaken us to the gift you have already given, and stir up the Spirit within us so that on Christmas Day we may sing with all our heart: "O come, let us adore him, Christ the Lord!"

A Joyful God

3rd Sunday of Advent   C

Zep 3:14-18
Phil 4:4-7
Lk 3:10-18

One word dominates today's readings: *Rejoice!* That is a very welcome word. All of us would rather have a good time than be miserable, and all of us enjoy a party more than a funeral. Besides, rejoicing is our destiny for all eternity because the Lord has promised us a heaven where every tear will be will be wiped away. And it is good to know that heaven does not begin on the other side of the grave. It is here now; here its joy already begins.

But suppose that after hearing today's readings and after having lived two whole weeks of Advent, we look into our hearts and must admit honestly, if ruefully, that we are not happy, not rejoicing. What then?

A couple of answers are possible. Maybe we are attempting to squeeze all our Advent preparation into a couple of Sunday Masses. But, as important as each Mass is, the time we give to tasting God's gifts to us may simply not be enough. One hundred and sixty-seven hours of worldliness may be too heavy for one hour of celebration.

Or perhaps we have been extremely careful in our Advent preparation. We have been coming to daily Mass, have been following customs like the Advent wreath at home, and have been praying the Scriptures—and we are still without the joy to which Paul calls the Philippians. No reason yet for us to despair. We still have two weeks more of Advent, and the Lord may be quietly plowing the still hard soil of our hearts and planting a seed whose sweet fruit we will taste in due time.

Lord, you have given us already the gift of yourself, and we rest in confidence that every one of your gifts will follow. You withhold nothing from us, Lord. We are sure that joy is always your final gift to us, so overpowering and so glorious that Paul can only say:

Eye has not seen, ear has not heard,

    nor has it so much as dawned on man
what God has prepared for those
    who love him! (1 Cor 2:9).
   Lord, Zephaniah says it beautifully. He writes
that the Father "will sing joyfully because of you"
(Zep 3:17b). Lord, let this vision of a joyful, singing
God enter deeply into us, and let our hearts sing with
him!

Christ-Bearers

4th Sunday of Advent   C

Mi 5:1-4
Heb 10:5-10
Lk 1:39-45

   Our celebration of Christ's coming to us is now
only days away, and the Church gives us today a portion
of the perennially thrilling story of his birth. Today
Mary is the central figure of the Gospel. And the way
Luke presents her tells us what these Advent weeks
have been all about.
   For Mary is presented today as a Christ-bearer. She
is one to whom the most glorious thing has already happened, but one also for whom even greater things are
yet to come. Mary already carried the Lord with her
when she visited Elizabeth; and Elizabeth knew it. In
her words of greeting, she became the first to fulfill
Mary's prophecy that all generations would call her
blessed. And the woman the Father had blessed with
Christ's presence brought a blessing to Elizabeth. Even
the baby in her womb leapt with joy.
   Blessing, blessing, blessing—the whole story of
Christ's coming to us, and Mary is right in the middle of
it. And the story is not yet finished.

   Lord Jesus, your mother is so close to us. Each of
us has also received great blessing: Each of us bears you
within us. Even greater things are in our future, for none
of us has yet brought you to fullness within us.
   All through Advent we have asked to grow in

awareness of your gift to us so that we can celebrate it fittingly on Christmas day. Even when that day comes, we know we still have many Christmases ahead of us before your likeness is apparent in us. But like your Mother, we are within your circle of blessedness. Finish growing within us, we pray.

Helpless in Human Hands	Is 52:7-10
	Heb 1:1-6
Christmas—Mass During the Day	Jn 1:1-18

What an important and happy day today is! Important because we celebrate the most unlikely of all paradoxes: God becoming man and making his dwelling among us. Happy because he comes as an infant, without force, to bring us the most satisfying of all revelations: that our God is a Father.

In his humanity, the Son reveals the Father by everything he is and does. He is the very Word of the Father. And so we see him in the manger—and we see God's willingness to be helpless in human hands. We remember his changing water into wine, healing, forgiving sin—and we see the Father's intimate care for his children.

It is important that we understand Jesus as the Father's Word. We must not be deaf to him, because deafness here is deadly. It would be a case not only of not hearing Jesus, but also of not hearing him whom he expresses. While it is true that every creature speaks something of the Father, it is also true that none of them completely conveys him. That is Jesus' job.

Today, Lord, we celebrate you as the final and satisfying Word the Father speaks to us. We want to hear you, Lord, because if you can begin your explanation of the Father with the loveliness of Bethlehem and climax it with the self-giving of Calvary, our God must be lovely indeed. Lord Jesus, Word of God, God-with-us, we praise you, love you and worship you on this, your birthday!

A Gift of Love

Sir 3:2-6, 12-14
Col 3:12-21
Lk 2:41-52

Holy Family
Sunday in the Octave of Christmas   C

Many different kinds of families come together to make up our parish community. Some are newlyweds still discovering each other; others are elderly couples whose faithfulness and love have refined their faces with a loveliness no makeup can give. Some live in large and noisy households; others live alone in the aching loneliness of widowhood or the independence of the single life. Every Sunday they all gather to become one family in Christ.

A church full of families is a church filled with love. That is not to say it is not also a church full of people who have argued and hurt one another, been selfish and cruel to each other. Very few families exist without these strains. But, thankfully, very few families exist *on* fights, either. The air clears, sanity returns and the permanent bonds of love reassert themselves. The family is the everyday experience of God's love.

Lord, keep our families secure in the bonds of love. Where there is anger and division, bring your healing. Where there is love and forgiveness, let your peace remain. With our hearts we embrace the families which produced us and the families which sustain us. Thank you for this gift of love.

Real Treasure Nm 6:22-27
Gal 4:4-7
Octave of Christmas Lk 2:16-21
Solemnity of Mary, Mother of God

The Lord once said, "Where your treasure is, there your heart is also" (Mt 6:21), a sentiment with which we can easily sympathize. Those of us who have our money sunk in a portfolio of stock know what it is to wait for the financial pages of the daily newspaper. Those of us who are investing 20 years of our life in paying off a house know how much we would grieve at losing it. These things are our treasures, and they draw our hearts and thoughts like magnets.

It is interesting to see where Mary's treasure was. The angel's news of miraculous pregnancy, Joseph's trust and the trip to Bethlehem, the birth, the visits of shepherds and Magi, and the flight to Egypt: all these events and so many others were Mary's treasure. In her heart she reflected on them. And they must have formed her person deeply and permanently.

For all these events and all her thoughts about them centered on the Lord, and when he becomes the center of anyone's life, amazing and beautiful things happen. He was all of Mary's treasure. She was so centered on him that she could eventually summarize everything she would ever say to anybody about him to the waiters at Cana: "Do whatever he tells you" (Jn 2:5). That is a glorious simplification of values into one value that is all-embracing. It makes all the sense in the world, and it is another sign of what an important model Mary is for all of us.

Lord, you have touched us too, each one of us. But we are too insensitive to you. You give us life, and we do not know it. You give us love, and we do not feel it. Every day of our lives you stand at our doors and knock, and we do not open. Lord, Mary is not different from us in your fundamental gift of yourself to her. But she is different from us in treasuring you, thinking of

you and centering her whole life on you. Lord, make us like Mary. Open our eyes and our hearts to our real treasure—you.

Savoring the Feast

Sir 24:1-4, 8-12
Eph 1:3-6, 15-18
Jn 1:1-18

2nd Sunday After Christmas

Today we are now far enough removed from our celebration of the Lord's birthday to reflect on what Christmas meant to us this year. We know what it meant to the department stores: big sales. But we also know how quickly the stores and radio and TV switched Christmas off on December 26. Of course, there are post-Christmas bargains, but they have the embarrassed air of goods that have outlasted their welcome on the store counters.

How about us? Did we switch Christmas off just as abruptly? Did we, as our bloodshot eyes watched the last minute of the last Christmas TV special, say to our groggy family, "Well, another Christmas gone. Back to work tomorrow"? We sometimes cram Christmas into the few days right before December 25. No wonder that the day is sometimes a letdown for us and that the days that follow echo almost no resonance from the feast.

The Lord knows and would have us know too that Christmas is no celebration to be rushed through in department-store hopping and tree-trimming. It is rather a time for quiet prayer about his becoming one of us. But that supposes we have some sense of his grandeur as God and of our own fragility and sinfulness. We simply will have none of that sense without taking time. We had four weeks to prepare for Christmas, but the Father prepared the world for thousands of years to receive his son. We have a few weeks after Christmas to taste the depths of this mystery, but the whole world has not absorbed it in almost 2,000 years.

Lord, Christmas is a powerful, adult, demanding mystery. Before the season ends, bring us to prayer on what Christmas is and clear our heads of the tinsel of a surface celebration. Lead us to the wonder of the gift you are, and prepare us to return to you the gift you want from us: ourselves.

Rise Up!   Is 60:1-6
                                                     Eph 3:2-3, 5-6
Epiphany   Mt 2:1-12

So much demands our attention on the feast of the Epiphany: the openness of the astrologers, the defensiveness of Herod, the obvious conviction of Matthew that in Jesus the promises of the Old Testament were fulfilled beyond anybody's expectation. But perhaps we ignore too often the implications of Isaiah's cry to Jerusalem: "Rise up in splendor!" (Is 60:1a).

Isaiah is speaking to us. For while this feast celebrates the first signs of the glory that is the Lord's, it also celebrates what that glory means for us who believe. He is never only God-made-flesh; he is always God-made-flesh-for-us. The glory that shines on his face is meant to lend radiance to ours, too.

Today we celebrate the beauty of a people who have opened themselves to the presence of the Father and of the Spirit in the Word. And that people includes us. Where once we were blind, now we see. Where once the whispers of the hidden God could not penetrate the noise of the world in which we were immersed, now our ears have been opened to a human voice inviting us to come to the Father.

Lord Jesus, today we celebrate some of the consequences of your coming in the stillness of the night to pitch your tent among us. Those consequences are in each of us, and in all of us as your people.

We thank you for yourself and we thank you for

your word to us. We thank you for the almost 20 centuries of believing persons who have brought you to us and with whom we stand in our witness to you. We thank you for the Church, the new Jerusalem; and today we heed Isaiah's cry because, Lord, you have given the Church the splendor of your presence. We worship you!

The Gift of New Life Is 42:1-4, 6-7
Acts 10:34-38
Baptism of the Lord   C Lk 3:15-16, 21-22

It is amazing how we have domesticated Baptism. Most of us were baptized when we were infants, and for that touch of divinity on our budding lives we are, of course, thankful. But we did not have to do much to be baptized. Our godparents brought us to the church, the priest sprinkled water on us, and we received the stupendous gift of being buried to sin and of rising with Christ to a life that would never end. But we wonder whether we have ever really appreciated what happened to us on our baptismal day. We did not have to go through the long preparation adults must endure when they become Christians. All we had to do was be born and be brought to church. The Lord is indeed lavish!

But the gift asks for consequences. And we are far from sure that we pay them. If indeed our Baptism was a death to sin, why are our lives so stained by our personal sins? If we have risen to new life, why are we so much more fascinated by this passing scene than we are in the landscape Jesus has opened to us? We are a new creation. But some of us live our lives as if Baptism had never happened, and perhaps most of us have never committed ourselves completely to living the new life. We have never become what we really are.

Somewhere in our lives we have to make our own what has already happened to us. Somewhere and sometime we will have to say: "I am a child of God; I must join the family circle; I must allow God really to be my

Father." In a word, we must become the Christians we already are.

So why do we hesitate? Is it, Lord, that we do not pray enough? Is it that we have no counterweight to the brutal force the world can exert on us? Is it that we expect the ceremony of Baptism to save us? But ceremony saves no one. *You* save everyone who will receive your mercy and respond to it.

Lord, on this day when we celebrate your baptism, let us celebrate also our own. Give us the nudge we need to live as if we were seeking Baptism and not as if we had forgotten we had ever received it.

A Season for Joy Jl 2:12-18
2 Cor 5:20—6:2
Ash Wednesday Mt 6:1-6, 16-18

We are not sure that we enjoy seeing this day arrive. Lent can seem so grim if we think it has to do with the frequent use of *no: no* to entertainment, *no* to food, *no* to wasting time, *no* to sin. But maybe we should pay more attention to the Gospel admonition to wear a happy face (Mt 6:17). In other words, Lent does not have to seem like a gray and creeping ghost. Much depends on why we do what we do during these days.

If we do nothing, we duck the whole issue. Our days during Lent will be as undistinguished now as they have always been. If Lent brings no change of perspective and practice, we are saying, in deed if not in words, that we don't need the Lord's mercy because we have not sinned. But we could not be more incredibly wrong.

Lord, help us, please, to see that only some sense of our own personal sin and our need for you makes Lent mean something to us.

If we do fill our lives with no's during these weeks, let us always understand that death to ourself and to our sin is never the only reason for our Lent. When we were baptized, we were baptized not only into your death and but also into your new life. Dear Lord, let our penances be colored with the light of Easter, as well as with the taking up of our cross and climbing our own Calvary. Then our Lent will have a joy that the world can never give!

Tempted Like Us

1st Sunday of Lent   C

Dt 26:4-10
Rom 10:8-13
Lk 4: 1-13

It is well to begin this Lent thinking and praying about temptation. We certainly have enough of it in our lives, and so we are comforted when we read that the Lord underwent this same unsettling experience. The difference between him and us is that he said no to temptation; many times we do not. But his temptations were as real as ours, as attractive and as probing in showing the kind of persons we really are. If we think that the Evil One had absolutely no chance with Jesus and that Jesus had the easiest time in the world defeating him, we deny the Incarnation.

No, his temptations tested him in his full manhood, in his passions, ambitions and sense of independence. And if we ever think that his temptations were little games he played with the Evil One just to show how we must act, we ignore both the power of evil and the fragility of anyone who is human. At no time did Jesus underestimate the power of malice and of evil. Perhaps his struggle against it had an urgency our weak resistance hardly ever has. For who among us has resisted the sinful call of our flesh to the extent that the struggle made us sweat drops like blood?

Lord, you did indeed struggle with temptation—in the desert, at Gethsemane, and most powerfully in the loneliness of the cross where your sense of having been forsaken made you cry out to the Father.

Lord Jesus, temptation is never sin. Temptation is an invitation to sin. But that does not mean that it cannot frighten and upset us until we wonder whether your Father has left us alone against the malevolence of all that is not good. Any contact with real evil is horrifying, Lord, even when it comes, as it often seems to, smiling and beckoning us to a good we know we must not have.

Lord, we know we will not escape temptation. We know too that temptation has its allies in our own hearts. Save us from ourselves, Lord. Without you, we are lost.

Homesickness

2nd Sunday of Lent   C

Gn 15:5-12, 17-18
Phil 3:17—4:1
Lk 9:28-36

On a trip to Europe, the Grand Canyon or a particularly lovely place closer to home we have wondered at the beauty the Father has lavished on our world. We have even wondered what it would be like to live in such a spot. And yet something within us tugs more compellingly than our wonder. We take a last look, and come back again to that little piece of earth, lovely or not, that we call home. Home is where we belong.

"But the Son of Man has nowhere to lay his head" (Mt 8:20). The Lord had no home; he always wandered. He too liked the loveliness he saw in the delicacy of flowers and the gold of fields ready for harvest; but he stayed nowhere permanently. He ate in strangers' houses. He even made his family so all-embracing that the idea of home became impossible. He wanted everyone to be his brother or sister. No one place on this earth was his home, and no line of blood could restrict his family.

That is why the transfiguration was as much a temptation for Peter as it was a revelation. He was so overjoyed and so sure that he was now seeing Jesus in all that he would ever be that he wanted to stay forever on the mountain. He wanted to make a dwelling-place for the Lord. But Jesus said no to Peter. No place on earth was his final home, and Peter had to recognize that. No place would be his either. And no place is ours.

Lord Jesus, we pray today for a touch of homesickness. We ask to remember that the comforts of our home and family and our mutual love are not permanent. Death must come. No place on earth is our final home, no matter how shot through with heaven it is. We were made for you in *all* your glory. Lord, help us to want heaven!

Worthy in the Eyes of the Lord Ex 3:1-8, 13-15
1 Cor 10:1-6, 10-12
3rd Sunday of Lent   C Lk 13:1-9

Today's three readings are not for the self-righteous. And then again, maybe they are, more than for anybody else. For in the first reading, Moses is told to carry a promise to the Hebrew slaves to "lead them. . . into. . .a land flowing with milk and honey" (Ex 3:8b). But Moses could not fulfill that promise either for himself or for all but a few of those to whom he made it. Neither could he convince his people of the wonder of the promise. They did not see their liberation as an undeserved privilege; they rebelled and wanted to turn their backs on God. That's why Paul says: "God was not pleased with most of them" (1 Cor 10:5a).

That makes us wonder whether the Father could say the same thing about us. This is a healthy wonder, because it shows we do know we are sinful. The only ones among us who are almost incurably sick are the same ones Paul singled out for his last sentence in today's second reading: "Let anyone who thinks he is standing upright watch out lest he fall!" (1 Cor 10:12)

Only when we say, "I have no sin," do we cut ourselves off from God's mercy, perhaps because we are insulted to think that we need mercy. But we do. We only *think* we are standing upright. We do not see our sins, especially our failure to do what is loving and just. We pride ourselves on not doing what is wrong. But not doing what is wrong is only the beginning of uprightness; when we have ceased to do wrong, we must begin to do right. Until we do, we are not even off our bellies yet.

Lord, grant that none of us make that mistake. You have given each of us so much, and we do try to respond, even though we stumble. Our great joy is that you never give up on us, even if sometimes we almost give up on ourselves. But you know the good that is in us, you want us to cultivate it, and to bring forth the kind of fruit you know we can bear. Stay by us, Lord. Help us to continue to grow in your love, and to rejoice that you see so much in us that even Calvary did not stop you from winning us. Lord, through your eyes we see our worth!

A Family Affair

4th Sunday of Lent   C

Jos 5:9, 10-12
2 Cor 5:17-21
Lk 15:1-3, 11-32

Maybe the best story Jesus ever told was about the father and his two sons. He portrays a father who always keeps first things first, one son who put last things first until he learned a bitter lesson, and another son who never wandered far from dead center. And in showing us these three persons, the Lord shows us ourselves.

We are not always like the father who forgives everything and whose concern for his children is so great that he wants to leave no one out in the cold—no matter how much the person might deserve it. Still, enough of us have struggled with the problem of forgiving others that the father is a familiar figure. We know that nurturing a hatred is a bitter pleasure. And we know, at least sometimes, that casting out the devil of hardheartedness is sweet pain and lasting peace.

Nor are many of us like the riotous younger son. Most of us are peacefully domesticated. Still, when we feel those surges of anger within us, or when our body strains after someone we must not have, we know that the wild beast within us is tied by very fragile threads. We recognize in ourselves the younger son.

But, Lord, the majority of us can identify most easily with the elder son. Like him, we are always in your Father's home, and we never stray too far away. But also like him we often fail to appreciate our Father and what he is always giving us. And so we start totalling up what *we* have done for him. We see ourselves in some kind of fiscal relationship with him that can be represented on a balance sheet.

But, Lord, your Father is not our employer. And we are not wage-earners. Your Father is heading a family, not a factory, and all of us are sons and daughters around his table.

Lord Jesus, take the spirit of the elder son out of our hearts. We don't want to slave for your Father. We just want to love him and everybody else in the family.

Beyond Memory Is 43:16-21
Phil 3:8-14
5th Sunday of Lent   C   Jn 8:1-11

More than once we have asked the Lord to help us remember all that the Father has done for us. Memory is very important, because it makes us realize that what happens to us today is just one more sign of the graciousness that has always walked with us. When memory is grateful, the future is hopeful. And so we recall all that God did for Israel and the early Christians and the saints through the ages, and especially what he has done for each one of us—because each of us is a living history of the Father's warm and enduring love.

Still the readings of today's Mass invite us beyond memory. Paul and Isaiah both urge us to leave the past behind us. Memory is important, but it is not enough. If we live only by memory, we can forget that all the past is only a prologue to today. We can forget that all the Father's deeds for our ancestors are meant to show that he loves all his children, including us. We must not live only on what he did for Abraham and Moses, for Peter and Paul. We must also live on his personal love for each one of us now. From this point of view, we ought to forget the past, welcome the present and reach out to the future. For the Father is constantly doing something new!

Lord, your Father never stops doing something new in each one of us. We are too often insensitive to his constant loving touch, and so we can imagine this day a blank page in our personal history. Of course, the page is not blank; it is crowded, crammed, written across and up and down with your Father's love. That is why, Lord Jesus, we need to pray! And we need to pray not so much for his help, but that we might *know* he never fails to help us. We need time to be aware of your Father every day. We need to close our eyes, shut out the world and become alive to the constant newness your Father creates for us.

Lord, your kingdom is within us *now*. Help us not to miss it.

In Triumph and Defeat	Is 50:4-7
	Phil 2:6-11
Palm Sunday C	Lk 22:14—23:56

When we think about Jesus on the first Palm Sunday, we see so many similar situations in our own lives.

He enjoyed a temporary triumph when the people welcomed him into Jerusalem. Many of us have known the sweetness of a victory: a baby born in perfect health, a promotion in our job, a scholarship to a university. But also, like him, we know that no victory on this earth lasts forever. The jubilation evaporates and the routine of the everyday again claims us. This earth is not the scene for anything eternal; it is always just a prologue.

We also see the Lord today in his prayer of agony in the garden. In some ways he died twice during the terrible hours after the Last Supper. His prayer was the cry of a person who already felt the malice of the world tearing at his flesh, and so his sweat flowed like the blood that would well from his wounds the next afternoon. Jesus was afraid of Calvary. And we know—at least, a little—how he felt.

For we have suffered through the hours of waiting for an operation on our own bodies; we have felt our hearts miss a beat when the attendants came to wheel us to the operating room. We know the panic of waiting for anticipated pain and of wanting to escape. But we go, and not just to operating rooms; we go to all the crosses that our days of love and duty bring us. Human life is no picnic, and merely knowing that fact is not always a help.

Lord Jesus, we see you on your cross today. We see you die a real death—death with a dignity that the squalor of blood and dirt and jeers cannot touch.

No one of us has yet died. But we know that we will die. And we know that your dignity is not beyond us, because we have seen parents, children, spouses and friends accept the sentence against them and pass through the gate of death with you in their hearts and on their lips. We are sure that our last moments, too, can be tinged with triumph. For we are never alone, Lord. You are one with us in all our sufferings and our joys, our death and our triumph.

A New Day

Easter Sunday

Acts 10:34, 37-43
Col 3:1-4 or 1 Cor 5:6-8
Jn 20:1-9

"This is the day the Lord has made"! (Ps 118:24a) All the agony of Gethsemane and Calvary, all the exhausting waiting of Holy Saturday is over. On the cross, the Lord pronounced it finished; and so it was. And yet, in an absolutely fantastic sense, it was all just beginning.

This day is Easter! It is the Lord's new life we celebrate today. We no longer see him as we saw him on Good Friday or on any of the days before. We see him today the way Mary Magdalene and the disciples on the road to Emmaus saw him: as one whom they had known but who has now become so much more. We see the Lord as one who works among us unseen until he pronounces our names, as one who walks with us unknown until he breaks bread for us.

Lord Jesus, Easter is your day, but in your typically generous way you make it our day too. For you did not begin your new life so only you could be a conquerer of death. You began it so that you could give your victory to each one of us. And your new life has none of the limits of the old; place or time will never again limit your presence. Your "where" is everywhere, your "when" is now. All we need do to welcome you is turn to you, for you are always turned to us.

Lord Jesus, we give you praise and glory for your risen life with us! You have gone before us to prepare the way, to prepare a place for us. You invite us to come to you, to bring all that cries out for healing and refreshment, and to find comfort in you. Your resurrection is the victory over all that threatens to defeat us. Today, Lord, we know that we will win. How can we lose? We have you!

The Creation of a Family Acts 5:12-16
Rv 1:9-11, 12-13, 17-19
2nd Sunday of Easter   C Jn 20:19-31

John, the author of the book of Revelation, expresses to us a most profound Easter truth: that the Lord's triumph is complete. He reigns now over a kingdom in which every tear is wiped away. The ancient enemies, sin and death, are no longer in control; theirs is not the final answer to why we were born. They may still struggle against his goodness; we might sin, and we do sin, and we all will die. But we bring our sin to the Lord, and he erases it; we die in him, and he swallows our death in his new life. All that he has won, he has won for us.

And so, Lord, John can call himself our brother, sharing in the victory you have won. And so is every other person who has ever died in you, because all of us have one life: yours. So, too, is each person a brother or sister to every other person. We know, Lord, the consequences of these family ties, and we want to do what we can to respect them.

We thank you for the generous people among us who show us what a real family we are: those who open their hearts and wallets to the poor of the town and the world, those who spend their time visiting shut-ins, those who gather to tend the property of the old, those who give their professional services free to people who cannot pay—in a word, Lord, those who love. That is what Easter is all about, too: the creation of a family.

Signs of His Presence Acts 5:27-32, 40-41
Rv 5:11-14
3rd Sunday of Easter   C Jn 21:1-19

At the shrine of Lourdes or Fatima or St. Anne de Beaupré can be seen the crutches left behind by people who have been cured. Those crutches are quiet testimony to the Lord's desire that sin and all its consequences be removed from his world. And some of us have seen the Sacrament of the Anointing of the Sick and the laying on of hands bring relief from pain—and even outright cures. We have been, perhaps, a bit frightened by these signs of the Lord's interest in us.

That kind of sign opens our eyes to the Lord. He used them often when he walked the earth; and he told his apostles to go and cure every kind of illness—and they did. But we also must face the truth that for every person who has witnessed a miracle, there are many more who have not. That disproportion may be because most of us have never asked for enough; we may be too like the townsfolk for whom Jesus could work no miracles because of their lack of faith.

If that is the case, Lord, then today we ask again that you increase our faith. We need to use the power at our fingertips.

But perhaps, Lord, you give us the faith to see you in the more ordinary signs of your constant presence among us, something like the way you showed yourself to your apostles as they worked at their job of catching fish. These men had already seen you after your resurrection, and they might have been expected to walk around starry-eyed and completely changed. Yet here they were back in the boats, heaving out nets, sweating, and about as successful as they had been when you first met them. And you came to them again. The daily grind and, in the midst of it, you.

That scene appeals to us, Lord. The fabric of our lives is the ordinary. When the extraordinary happens, fine—it is a sign. But it is a sign of what is always happening: you among us, quietly and lovingly at work. Lord Jesus, thank you!

Courage in Our Hearts

4th Sunday of Easter   C

Acts 13:14, 43-52
Rv 7:9, 14-17
Jn 10:27-30

Watching a heavyweight fight on TV, we wonder at the endurance of the boxers. We listen to excited commentators praise the courage of the two men, and we must admit that the fighters are doing what most of the rest of us would be afraid to do. But some of us can still wonder, "To what purpose?" The answer is, of course, money and fame, two powerful motives. People do a lot of strange things to get them.

But money and fame are not the only things people are willing to suffer for. Men are amazed at the courage in the hearts of women before and during childbirth. Even when they are with them during the moments of delivery, they sense the essential loneliness of these women, and they can only guess at the pain new life exacts. At moments like these, money and fame are trivial considerations; much more important realities are at issue.

People today are still full of courage in matters of truth and justice and honesty. Russian Jews and Lithuanian Catholics are serving prison terms because they asked for basic human rights. Priests are silenced in South Africa because they challenged the validity of repressive laws. Missionaries are dead in Rhodesia because they would not leave areas dominated by terrorists. Courage in high matters like these still moves us.

And, Lord, courage has to be in our hearts too. The readings from the Acts of the Apostles for the last two weeks are full of the truth that your gifts demand consequences. The apostles were persecuted, but they remained firm. We hear these readings and ask, "Where is the courage in my life as a Christian?"

Lord, we may not be persecuted, but we must still have courage to withstand the contemptuous smile, to speak the word that must be said, to take the position that must not be ducked, to live a Christianity that must

be more than ritual. Lord, we must have courage.
Strengthen us.

The Heart of the Message	Acts 14:21-27
	Rv 21:1-5
5th Sunday of Easter C	Jn 13:31-33, 34-35

We ask for courage, because our weakness in the face of a hostile or contemptuous world betrays the Lord. But courage is not the ultimate reaction he wants from us. His final command to us was not to be brave, but to love as we are loved. We need courage to love the way he loved, but courage and strength must be tempered with understanding and compassion if we are to be saved from the temptation to solve our problems the way the world does: by a brutal fist and a relentless severity. Courage is the *servant* of love.

And so we realize the wisdom of the Lord's prediction: that we will be known as his disciples by our love for one another. How simple that is! Our parish will be known as a group of Christ's disciples when we love one another. It is not our church building nor our school nor our packed Sunday Masses nor our strong stands on controversial issues that will do it.

Paul recognized the priorities when he assured the Corinthians that without love, even undergoing martyrdom would be an empty act. The whole world saw the witness of the first martyrs as so powerful that the saying was born: "The blood of the martyrs is the seed of the Church." And yet their deaths were not the ultimate witness; love was and is.

Lord, what is your judgment on our parish? Can we be recognized by others as your real disciples? The test is simple: Do we love one another? Can we lift up our heads on Sunday morning and see in the congregation people in whom we have made a heavy investment of our life and love and care and concern? Or do we see a building full of strangers?

Lord, we want the heart of your message. We want to love and to do all the works love asks. Help us!

Together in the Church

6th Sunday of Easter   C

Acts 15:1-2, 22-29
Rev 21:10-14, 22-23
Jn 14:23-29

Once in a while we hear someone say: "I don't need the Church; I can pray to God and worship him on my own. I don't need the hassle of all that institutional organization." There is a certain appeal in that simple stance. But none of us would even know the name of God without hearing it first from someone else. Each person is born into a society with or without belief in some kind of God, and each person agrees with or modifies or denies that belief. We depend on one another to teach us belief and we all receive so much from one another in this matter of God. When we finally do understand that we, in some sense, give God to each other, then we will begin to see the folly of a God-and-I-alone stance and begin to appreciate the value of the Church.

The Church is the gathering of people who believe in Christ and hand on that belief to others. All the readings from the Acts of the Apostles during this Easter season show the infant Church as it tries to understand its duties and its rights. Today's, for example, shows the Church making a very important decision for its new members. The point is that new members came into the group, and the group welcomed them.

And nothing has changed. If we want to be true believers, we must still belong to the believing community, and the group must still receive us. Anything we pick up outside finds resonance and meaning within the group of believers. And all of this is so because the Lord planned it that way. He was the one who selected the apostles and sent them into the world. Anyone who hears them hears Jesus. It simply does not work any other way.

Lord Jesus, help us to love the Church, not only because it is the group in which we find those who believe in you; but also because in it we find *you*. You are the Lamb in the holy city both of heaven and of the Church. You built the Church on the 12 courses of stones that we call the Apostles, and you fit each of us into the great city you are building. Lord, we need the Church. Do not let us ever forsake it, and do not let us think we can ever do without it.

Bringing the Seed to Full Flower   Acts 1:1-11
Eph 1:17-23
The Ascension   C   Lk 24:46-53

The meaning of today's feast is reflected in the second reading. Paul prays that his Ephesians may recognize two great truths. The first concerns the Lord: The Father has raised Jesus from the dead and placed him at his right hand in heaven above every other created reality. And that is one tremendous significance of the Ascension—Jesus entering into the triumph won by his life of integrity and his obedient death. We celebrate today the glory of the Christ we shall know forever: victorious and immortal, powerful and glorious, the conqueror of everything that is evil and mortal, and the joy of everything that is good.

The second thing that Paul prays that his Ephesians may recognize concerns themselves—and us, too. He asks the Father to enlighten us that we may know the hope given each of us because of Christ. Paul calls it a glorious heritage and an immeasurable exercise of the Father's power. In other words, Paul prays that we may have the vision to see that our whole existence is now bound up in Christ and destined for the existence he now has.

We celebrate not only you today, Lord; we also celebrate ourselves. Where you are, we shall be. And in some mysterious way, not only "shall be," but already are. For you are our head and we are your members. Your triumph is already ours. The power your Father showed in raising you and exalting you is already at work in us. We are already in heaven in hope, and we are asked to bring a bit of heaven to earth by our lives.

Lord, you told us that you would lose no one that your Father had given you. That is gloriously consoling. Help us to believe deeply in your promise, in your Father's power, in the hope we have received as our consolation and in the heaven which awaits us. Lord, bring to full flower the seed of life you have already planted in us.

Bound in Love

7th Sunday of Easter   C

Acts 7:55-60
Rv 22:12-14, 16-17, 20
Jn 17:20-26

We see around us all sorts of groupings of people. Sometimes the people in them want to be together; sometimes not. Prisons certainly have people who live together, but they hardly want to stay together. We see the same in hospitals or motels, on trains or airplanes. People come together in these places for a while, perhaps become friendly, but are never satisfied to say, "This is my home and these are my friends." The reason is, of course, that all these places are way-stations in our travel to someplace else and to people we have bound more intimately into the fabric of our lives.

There are other groupings of people who really do want to stay together. A young bride and groom pledge to stay together until death parts them. Many families know first the joy of loving closeness while the children grow and then the joy of union in spirit when the children scatter to build their own families. And we all know the bonds of friendship.

All these groupings are signs of the closeness for which the Lord prays in today's Gospel. Even the involuntary groups are signs, faint though they are. But much better are the groups which know love as their binding force. These show that what he asks for is an attainable reality, one that is the best of realities.

You pray, Lord, that we might be one—our unity mirroring the bond between you and the Father. You ask for something amazing: that all of us may be as committed to one another as you are to your Father and as both of you are to the Holy Spirit. That is why we need all the signs you give us that such a unity is possible. That is why we need loving and faithful husbands and wives and generous and open families and neighborhoods. We know the happiness in these groups, and we know that nothing is better than that happiness. And when we hear you say to all of us, "Be one," we hear you say, "Be completely and unendingly happy."

No wonder, Lord, that our unity in this parish is the best advertisement for our Catholicism. You said it would be. It has to be. It is the living fulfillment of your greatest commandment.

Waiting and Ready　　　　　　　　Acts 2:1-11
　　　　　　　　　　　　　　　　　1 Cor 12:3-7, 12-13
Pentecost　　　　　　　　　　　　Jn 20:19-23

We are not too different from those people who were waiting in the upper room for something to happen. They had heard the Lord's words and liked what they heard; and so have we, or we wouldn't gather on Sunday. They were amazed at Christ's love and life and death; and we too wonder how and why he did what he did. All of them, except a few women and one man, were frightened by the cross and fled from it; and the Lord knows how many times we have done the same.

Perhaps the big difference between that group in

the upper room and us is that they wanted to be different; they really wanted something better than their cowardliness, but they did not know what. And so they were waiting and they were ready.

Our problem is that most of us are *not* waiting; or, if we are, it is for a better job or a better house, or for something else whose value is limited by the breath we draw.

Lord, too many of us are not waiting for you. When you knock at our door, we have our radios and TV's and telephones going and so we can't hear you. But we thank you, Lord, for never leaving us, even when we have left you. You never lose patience; you never give up; you never walk away. You know we are in there someplace.

Our prayer this Pentecost Sunday is a simple and humble one: Awaken in us a discomfort about our lives; awaken in us a desire for a Spirit greater than our own; shake us out of our self-satisfaction. Make us want you, wait for you, welcome you when you come. Make us ready for our own personal Pentecost.

Doctrine or Experience?

Prv 8:22-31
Rom 5:1-5
Jn 16:12-15

Trinity Sunday
Sunday After Pentecost   C

Perhaps the mystery of the Holy Trinity is *too* much of a mystery for us. We are taught that God is one nature and three persons; that the Father is neither begotten nor proceeds from anyone; that the Son is begotten by the Father; and that the Holy Spirit proceeds from both the Father and the Son. But the language and perhaps even the ideas leave most of us unmoved. We nod our heads in agreement; we believe. But our belief in the mystery of the Holy Trinity has little impact on how we live our lives at home or work or school.

And yet to the Lord, the Father and the one he sent after his Ascension were his whole life. They were not just an intellectual exercise; they were real to him— so real that Jesus spent whole nights praying to the Father. And he consoled his friends when he was about to leave them by promising them someone who would be as important to them as he had been. And that promise was fulfilled. The Holy Spirit came and swept them off their feet in the upper room.

So, Lord, our problem is that we don't know the Father the way you knew him. We don't experience the Spirit the way the apostles and Mary experienced him. But without that kind of knowledge and experience the Holy Trinity does remain too much of a mystery for us.

On this feast of the Holy Trinity, Lord, help us to allow God our Father really to be a Father for us and to us; and help us to open our hearts to the Spirit of light and love. And help us to know you, too, because you opened the way to the Father and together sent us your Holy Spirit to be with us forever.

Liking the Lord　　　　　　　　　　　Gn 14:18-20
　　　　　　　　　　　　　　　　　　　　　1 Cor 11:23-26
Corpus Christi　C　　　　　　　　　　　Lk 9:11-17

How often have we received the Lord in the sign of bread and wine? Many of us come to the altar every Sunday. That means that in the last year he has come to us 52 times; some of us receive more often than that. Fifty-two meetings with the Lord should make a difference in our lives. We don't even see some of our best friends that often, and they certainly have shaped our lives in many ways. They influence us because they are important to us, and we respect their opinions and values. In other words, we like them.

Lord, do we like *you*? We often say in our prayer,

"Lord, I love you, I adore you, I worship you." And we try to mean it. But do we *like* you?

When you come to us in the bread and wine, we can turn away from you so quickly, perhaps even before we have returned to our seats. Or when we are in our seats we close our eyes and try to concentrate on you and within a minute or two we are thinking of the Sunday roast or the afternoon ride or the job trouble that won't go away. So often, Lord, we go to Holy Communion and we receive a sacrament—but we are not affected enough by you. And yet every sacrament is nothing if it is not a meeting with you.

So, there you are, always dependable, always present, always offering yourself. And here we are, receiving you and not really welcoming and being influenced by you. Lord, we ask you today: Help us to understand what Holy Communion is all about; help us to want you and what you want. Help us to let you be our friend. Help us to like you.

Many Gifts　　　　　　　　　　　Is 62:1-5
　　　　　　　　　　　　　　　　　　1 Cor 12:4-11
2nd Sunday　C　　　　　　　　　　　Jn 2:1-12

The apostle Paul says to his quarrelsome Corinthians in today's second reading something that we of today's Church could heed. Paul tells a Church that had been richly blessed with all types of gifts to remember that every gift has been given by the Holy Trinity, and that no gift has been given for any one person alone. Every gift is for ministry to the whole group; no one can clutch a grace to himself or herself and say: "Look how much God loves me. I am not like other people."

The Lord has raised so many new opportunities for ministry in today's Church. He has invited all of us to join our priests and religious in the work of revealing his presence in every neighborhood. Lay people are called to serve as teachers and administrators, at liturgy and in civic affairs and in many other ways. He invites us in this blessed but chaotic time to stir up the Spirit that has always been ours and to rejoice in the truth of Paul's words: "To each person the manifestation of the Spirit is given for the common good" (1 Cor 12:7).

Lord, let us not look only at other people when we examine ourselves on what Paul is saying. Let us first look at ourselves to discover the gifts you have given for the common good. Do we see them, and do we use them? Is our talent multiplying itself, or have we buried it in the ground somewhere? Help us, Lord, to praise you when others in the parish offer their gifts. Let us encourage them when they do, and never carp, criticize or humiliate them. Lord, you want us today to open our eyes to your working through people. Help each of us to pray for clearer vision.

We Are One Body

3rd Sunday   C

Neh 8:2-4, 5-6, 8-10
1 Cor 12:12-30
Lk 1:1-4; 4:14-21

The three readings of today's Mass are linked by a common theme: the unity of a people hearing God, hoping in his promises, and being open to his Spirit.

In the first reading Ezra reintroduces the Jewish people to the Law, and so again makes them into a nation with its own God and its own way of life. The Law unified them, because they all saw it as the will of God; in hearing and doing his will they found the heart of their cohesiveness as a people. No wonder they wept as they listened; they were rediscovering not only the will of God but also one another. And no wonder that Ezra urged them to rejoice and to feast; to find the Lord and one's place in the world is no small treasure.

And in the Gospel Jesus works with those same realities. The people have come together to hear the Scriptures reaffirm all their hopes as a nation and as individuals. And he tells them that their hopes have not been in vain. At last that great yearning for a Messiah that united Jewish hearts is fulfilled. God is ready to crown the people's fidelity with a victory so complete that in the chosen people all nations could count themselves blessed.

Paul tells us today what that victory meant. It was not the political and national independence the people had come to expect. It was an outpouring of the Spirit upon anyone who was willing to be open enough to receive it. And that Spirit does for us what it does for Jesus and the Father: It unites us in a living unity of love that Paul says is so intimate that we become one body.

Lord Jesus, make us appreciate the unity we have with you and with one another. Help us to see the silliness of some of the issues we fight about. Grant us hearts open enough to know the wisdom of the old advice to strive for unity in essentials, liberty in peripherals and love in all things. Do not allow us to squander the richness of the Spirit by indulging in contentiousness that divides and embitters us. We are one body, Lord. A body at war with itself simply makes no sense!

Partner in Love

4th Sunday   C

Jer 1:4-5, 17-19
1 Cor 12:31—13:13
Lk 4:21-30

The Church in these last few years has tried to become very sensitive to people who are receiving its sacraments. It has tried to give them a rich assortment of biblical texts to choose from as they prepare for each sacrament. And perhaps no text is chosen by young couples for their marriages more often than our second reading today. This is Paul's description of love. And a marriage filled with the love that Paul describes will indeed endure until death.

But young newlyweds have all their life yet to live. We who have been married for more than just a few months know that the strains of getting to know each other, of accommodating ourselves to each other, of forgiving burnt toast and weak coffee, forgotten anniversaries and angry words—we know that all these strains and thousands more like them make a patient and kind love very difficult. We know that a spouse's unexplained absence can arouse the green-eyed devil of jealousy. We know that we can fight with each other and brood over our hurt until healing becomes indescribably difficult.

We know all these strains, Lord, because we are two imperfect people exposing our weaknesses to each other and hurting one another even when we want most not to. Still, Lord, we cling together. And very probably you have more to do with that than we could possibly imagine. For we brought our wishes for a total married love to your altar, and we made you a partner in our lifelong union. You took our human love and made it an avenue of your daily entrance into our lives. In our love for each other, Lord, we give you to each other. And with you comes strength and peace and joy.

Lord, you have a great stake in our marriages. We thank you and bless you for your constant help!

A Generous Response

Is 6:1-2, 3-8
1 Cor 15:1-11
Lk 5:1-11

5th Sunday C

All parents know the puzzlement of seeing how different their children can be from one another. We all sometimes wonder why one child can be so ready to help, so willing to do what is asked, so cheery and bubbly and good-humored. Another can be so much the opposite: head like a rock, neck like iron, mouth always grave and unsmiling, and will seemingly set permanently on the "no" button. Why they are the way they are mystifies us. All we know is that the one is so agreeable to live with, and the other is a cross. We love him, but he is still a cross.

There is something lovable about the generous, openhearted, agreeable person. In today's three readings we meet a number of people like that. At the end of the first reading, Isaiah pictures himself as a child bouncing up and down in front of the Father, begging to be sent forth. And in the second reading Paul recalls with some shame what he had been before the Lord knocked him down. But the point is that when the Lord called him, he, like Isaiah, responded generously. In the third reading, three other men were just as willing to say yes to Jesus. Peter, James and John saw his power, heard his call and were completely convinced. They left everything to follow him.

Lord, each one of us can wonder: "What kind of person am I?" The agreeable, generous, ready person, or the everlasting no-sayer? If and when you call, what is my response? For, Lord, most of us have lived long enough to have fallen into habits of response, even if we are still children. Either you are finding us delightful to work with, or you are shaking your head over us, loving us, but still finding us a cross on your shoulders.

Lord, your first cross was heavy enough. Don't allow us to add to it. Help each of us to answer eagerly when you call.

Honest Answers

6th Sunday   C

Jer 17:5-8
1 Cor 15:12, 16-20
Lk 6:17, 20-26

Real prayer demands honesty before the Lord. Every now and then the Sunday readings underscore that demand. The Scripture is so insistent that we must face our own self-deception even before we pray. Today is such a day. Each of the readings invites us to be honest about our relationship with the Lord.

For example, Jeremiah holds out a curse to the one who trusts only human beings and a blessing to the one whose hope is in the Lord. When we really probe ourselves on that curse and that blessing, we can become worried. So many of us put so much trust in the companies we work for or the government which collects our social security taxes. We trust that our pension and our government benefits will protect us against the future. But that does not leave much room for trust in the Lord.

Or we hear Paul proclaim: "If our hopes in Christ are limited to this life only, we are the most pitiable of men" (1 Cor 15:19). What *are* our hopes in Christ? Are they only something we expect from him in this life, like peace or security? Or do we hope in one who lives and has brought us to life that lasts forever? It is a good set of questions, and honest answers to them can be very healthful.

Lord, in the Gospel we hear you bless people we might regard as cursed, and curse those to whom we always have the habit of giving respect and honor. For you bless the poor, the hungry and the sorrowing, and you threaten the selfishly rich and fat and convivial. And again we wonder how many of your values we have really made our own. Not many of us have thought it an honor to have a beggar at our table, but most of us would break our necks to host the richest man in town.

Lord, we have a long way to go, but thanks at least for giving us the honesty to be constantly starting on the way!

Infected with Worldliness   1 Sm 26:2, 7-9, 12-13, 22-23
1 Cor 15:45-49
7th Sunday   C   Lk 6:27-38

Our newspapers are full of events contrary to all that the Lord says in today's Gospel. He commands love of enemies, and we see accounts of terrorists killing government leaders and bombs ripping apart the innocent. He calls on us to turn the other cheek, and we hear about two factions in Northern Ireland letting no insult go unrevenged. He asks us to give a blessing when we are cursed, and we witness whole political movements based on hatred and destruction. Our world is sinful; it has never learned well what the Lord said in the Sermon on the Mount. It will invoke his name and celebrate his feasts like Christmas and Easter, but it does not really believe in him.

Perhaps the world thinks Jesus too visionary and impractical. But we know that the solutions the world proposes are hardly models of wisdom and are not very fruitful. As a writer early in this century said, "Christianity has not failed the world; the world has never tried it."

The question for each one of us is: "How much am I of the world?" The apostle Paul tells us that we cannot be taken out of the world. What we have to do is to take the world out of us.

Lord, Christian life in the midst of worldliness is not easy. Perhaps we will not be persecuted or thrown to the lions. But the raised eyebrow, the smug smile, the condescending question, and above all the prosperity of those who have made their terms with the world are sore temptations to us, especially when we find our own hearts yearning in the same directions.

Lord Jesus, your ways are bitter on the tongue. We find it very hard not to hit the person who hit us. Yet if all enmity would cease by our forbearance, how sweet it would be! Lord, we are infected with worldliness. Cure us.

Revealing Words

8th Sunday   C

Sir 27:4-7
1 Cor 15:54-58
Lk 6:39-45

Many of us have had the misfortune of being seated in a restaurant next to a table occupied by a real loudmouth. The trumpeting voice of the person can make milk curdle. But even worse is what the person might say. If he is repetitive, boastful or arrogant, critical, unkind or worldly—all these things are revealed in his words, and the people sitting nearby may eventually get irritated enough to ask for a more distant table. And all breathe a thanksgiving when he pays his bill and leaves.

Words can be frighteningly revealing. Today's readings emphasize that speech reveals the mind and heart. We can all say amen to that. All of us know how hard it is to hold our tongues when we know we should be quiet or hold fast a secret. A popular cartoon makes a joke about the "gossip fence," and we know that its modern version is the telephone.

Lord, what do our words reveal about ourselves? Have we criticized someone unjustly? Have we told someone's secret? Have we demeaned somebody's raise or good looks or good luck? Have we lacerated somebody's character? Words of this type not only hurt others, they show us ourselves, Lord.

But words also can excuse someone's brashness, defend a person's good name, warm a heart or praise another's goodness. Words are so cheap, Lord, and yet they purchase so much pain and so much pleasure. Help us to have a sweet spirit and to show it by a gentle tongue.

Remembering His Gifts

9th Sunday   C

1 Kgs 8:41-43
Gal 1:1-2, 6-10
Lk 7:1-10

Many of us have felt the gentleness of the Lord's presence and the kindness of his touch. Sometimes he uses a preacher to reveal his patient forgiveness and his yearning love. During a retreat he can be so real to us that we hate to receive the final blessing and go home again to our troubles and our jobs. In a prayer group his sweetness can overflow all boundaries till we know in our hearts the truth that "God is love" (1 Jn 4:16).

Perhaps we have had the astounding revelation of God's care in the recovery of someone we love from cancer, heart trouble or a serious operation. When we have prayed so fervently for God's help, the evidence of his love can cause us to praise and bless him in our gratitude.

And yet, Lord, we need to heed St. Paul's words in today's second reading, especially if we have not felt your closeness for awhile. He chides the Galatians for their quick desertion. Gracious feelings of thankfulness and praise do evaporate, and we find that the cure of a year ago has precious little effect on our relationship with you today. Perhaps, Lord, we find our spirit permeated by that devastatingly greedy and selfish axiom: "What have you done for me today?"

Lord, help us to understand how important remembering is when we approach you. Let us understand how vital it is for us to begin each session of prayer with a litany of your gifts to us. Let us grasp that your gifts reveal you—and you never change or go. Lord, let us want you more than your gifts!

Love Is the Name of God

10th Sunday C

1 Kgs 17:17-24
Gal 1:11-19
Lk 7:11-17

The first and third readings of today's Mass are lovely stories of God's care for the human relationships that are the fabric of our lives. The human beings with whom we live are important to us because the Father planned it that way. The Trinity lives in a family relationship of Father, Son and Infinite Love, and God wanted the humans he formed from the dust of the earth to mirror that relationship. The Genesis story of Adam and Eve has that wish of the Father as one of its most important features, for Eve was formed because Adam was lonely; she was presented to him as helpmate and wife.

But once we enter into relationships we learn the price that goes with an abandoning of selfishness and a growth in love. For love is not always a peaceful and ecstatic experience. Love can sometimes hurt. And it can especially hurt when it is subjected to the weakness of mortality. Our love for another human being springs from our heart of flesh, and that heart attains its immortality only through the experience of Calvary and Easter.

Our heart, even while it loves, knows the pain of watching those we love bear the weight of their own humanity. We may see our spouses suffer with a grave illness, be absent from us for long periods of time or even leave us in the definitive separation of death. Then we find that the more we have loved, the more terrible is our loss. But we also know that love is still our greatest treasure, no matter what suffering is involved. For not to love is to miss out on the most fully human and the most nearly divine of all the gifts God gives us.

Lord, in your restoring the dead son to his mother we see your care for human relationships. Teach us to care for them too and not to be afraid of love. Love is the name of God, and we are his children. Give us the confidence that heaven is family and friends and God.

In Need of a Nathan 2 Sm 12:7-10, 13
Gal 2:16, 19-21
11th Sunday   C Lk 7:36—8:3

It would not be the worst thing in the world for a Nathan to come into our lives occasionally to confront us saying, "Look, it's time to shape up! God has given you great parents, a fine home, a good education, a job that gives you enough to live on, a wonderful spouse, children who love you. But you fail to give the best of yourself to this family. You waste energy worrying about more money or a better house. You envy the neighbors' new car or patio or furniture."

Would our response to Nathan be like David's? David was an Oriental king, a breed that did not like being told they had sinned. John the Baptizer tried it and ended up without a head. But David listened, and his answer was the admission of the truth, "I have sinned against the LORD" (2 Sm 12:13b).

We, too, sin. And our sin is often remarkably like David's. Our sin is a forgetfulness of the blessings the Lord has heaped on us—and an even more radical forgetfulness that he is their source. We constantly tend to take all of our riches for granted. We say to ourselves, "I have worked hard; I deserve everything I have. And I'm going to get more." And yet Scripture stands against us and asks why we boast.

Lord, we are eternally Adam: We have Eden at our feet, and yet all we want is the apple of destruction. Open our eyes to our gifts and to you, their giver. Fill our hearts with thanks for you and for what you give. Douse our dizzy longings and set us at peace with what is ours.

Let us understand, Lord, that you are gracious love and that you want nothing for us but our best good. Let us be satisfied to say: "Your will be done." You said that to your Father in Gethsemane, and Mary said it to him in Nazareth. We could follow worse examples. And when we do, Lord, send us a Nathan!

Blind to Our Inheritance Zec 12:10-11
Gal 3:26-29
12th Sunday   C Lk 9:18-24

All of us have felt pity for a blind person. We see him tapping along with a white cane or led by a seeing-eye dog, and we say to ourselves: "He must miss so much." And yet, if we asked him, he might say, "I don't miss anything. How can I miss what I never knew?"

But he is not the only blind person in the world. Many, perhaps most of us, are blind—blind to the fact that we are sons and daughters of the Father. Does this truth make a great deal of difference in our lives? All we need do to test that is to ask ourselves what about our lives can be attributed to the fact that we are children of God? Is it gratitude? Or holiness? Or kindness to our brothers and sisters? Or joy because our Father is the great king?

And if that question is too abstract, maybe we should ask ourselves a simpler one: "What was the last thing I did simply because I was a child of God?" We might be humbled to find how blind we are to the dignity of our inheritance.

We live, Lord, as if our family tree began with somebody who first bore our family name. But it goes much farther back than any human ancestor. Our family is headed by your Father, and our inheritance is what he promises. But we are blind. And, worse, we don't even regret our blindness. How can we if we have never seen ourselves as his children? We cannot miss what we have never known.

Lord Jesus, richness, divine richness, presses in on us insistently the way light presses in on everything under the sun. Teach us to open our eyes. Increase our faith. Make our greatest joy a family joy: In you we are members of your Father's household. Lord, there and there alone is full joy.

Right Now

13th Sunday C

1 Kgs 19:16, 19-21
Gal 5:1, 13-18
Lk 9:51-62

Ingeniously we keep looking back after we have put our hands to the plow. Tomorrow is so much better a time to say yes to the Lord than today: We will be better prepared; we will have more time to pray; we will have things under better control. Perhaps we will straighten out a tangled marriage situation when our first child is ready for school or CCD. Maybe we will return to the sacraments when our little one receives his first Holy Communion. And it is possible that next year, when our job pressures are not so overwhelming, we will join that committee that will bring us into the service of others outside our home. But not today, not right now. We have so much to do; there are so many things that we simply have to do first.

And yet Simon left his nets immediately when the Lord invited him to follow. Matthew walked away from his desk in the tax office when Jesus called him. Paul, when he was knocked off his high horse, went where he was sent. The woman at the Samaritan well went to proclaim the Lord after her unsettling conversation with him. And the woman taken in adultery presumably heeded his advice to sin no more.

Lord, they were so ordinary—a fisherman, a civil service employee, a craftsman, a housewife, a sinner. But when you called, they answered, not with an easily-said yes, but with changed hearts and lives that made your values their own.

Lord, you call us in the words of Scripture and in the Bread we have received at Communion. Help us to open our ears and our hearts and our lives to you. We must learn that when you call us to follow, you always mean *now*.

Jerusalem, Our Joy

14th Sunday C

Is 66:10-14
Gal 6:14-18
Lk 10:1-12, 17-20

The first and the third readings today invite us to think about the Church, how we participate in it and how it affects us. In the first reading Isaiah sings one of his songs of consolation to the exiles and, in the Lord's name, promises them the great joy of knowing again the Jerusalem from which they had been exiled. He pictures Jerusalem as a mother eager to nourish them and to gather them into her arms.

Jesus' earliest followers, from Paul to the first readers of Revelation, regarded themselves as being in the new Jerusalem, the Church. It embraced them as Isaiah predicted the city on Zion would the homesick Jews. The Church should still be a home for us, a source of comfort and joy.

In the Gospel Jesus shows us the Church from another point of view. He sends his disciples out to carry on his work: proclaiming the Kingdom and overcoming evil. That must still be our essential task today, because we still are the Church. It is not a work that can be done easily and without danger; but it was not easy and it was certainly not safe for the Lord. And we must learn that the Church continues to be Jesus until he returns—in all his joy and suffering. It cannot be otherwise, because any other Church would betray him.

Lord, we look at ourselves today, and we ask two questions: "Is the Church a source of great joy for us?" and "Do we, the Church, proclaim you in the face of every evil around us?" We are not sure that we can answer yes to either question. Too often we see the Church as killing joy, not giving it; and too often our own participation in the Church is restricted to fulfilling obligations. Well, Lord, the two are tied together. No wonder we are not joyful. We have not entered into the heart of what the Church really is.

Lord, clutch our hearts to you. Help us to want

what you wanted. When together we speak your name without fear, when together we are willing to confront evil with good and human suffering with a healing touch, we will know your joy. Our Church will then mean something to us. It will be our home, our consolation.

The Law in Our Hearts

15th Sunday   C

Dt 30:10-14
Col 1:15-20
Lk 10:25-37

The story about the Good Samaritan today is very reassuring to us who are trying to live lives that make sense. The Samaritan was kind to the man clubbed by the robbers, not because of some grudging sense of duty but for the simple reason that he was moved by pity. He took care of the victim at some trouble and cost to himself. He became involved.

We have seen neighbors gather around a cancer-stricken person for months on end, helping with cleaning, laundry and meals, loving and caring until the person is mercifully released from suffering. We have seen old persons cared for by faithful visitors. We have seen families receive orphans into their midst as foster children or as possible adoptees. We have seen community collections for destroyed churches or stricken families.

Lord, we thank you for allowing us to see so much of that kind of human goodness around us. We have seen so many cases of people feeling sorry for other people and doing something about it.

Lord, we thank you for making our salvation so dependent on that type of feeling within us. Indeed, as Moses said, the law "is something very near" (Dt 30:14a). It is in our loving, caring human hearts. Help us, Lord, to continue to act on our good impulses. You built them into us, and you want us to use them.

Hospitable Hearts

16th Sunday   C

Gn 18:1-10
Col 1:24-28
Lk 10:38-42

One of the most reassuring promises the prophets made in the Old Testament was: "I will give them a new heart and put a new spirit within them; I will remove the stony heart from their bodies, and replace it with a natural heart. . ." (Ez 11:19).

Ezekiel wrote those words for a people who had become hard and standoffish and cruel to one another. The Father had not created them to be that way; they had manufactured a selfish, grasping society all by themselves. And the mess they had produced was not making anyone very happy, even those who were profiting most. Profit was the bitter fruit of a selfishness more arrogant and ruthless than their neighbor's. They could not be happy; they were too inhuman.

The heart God put into human beings is a heart made for love and care and help. It is a heart that rejoices in hospitality. It is a heart that welcomes friends and neighbors and strangers into its circle of warmth. Abraham and other desert nomads knew the joy of a heart like this, because they believed that in welcoming a stranger they might be entertaining God himself. And Mary and Martha knew its joy, too, because their home was open to Jesus, who had no place to lay his head.

Lord, help us too to have hospitable hearts. Let our family circles constantly grow larger as we welcome more and more friends into our homes. Teach us to make our parties, barbecues, outings and dances into events in which human hearts may grow. These times are so important in our lives; they are so joyful. You want them for us, and you bless them for us. In the midst of the people who gather in the name of friendship, you are forming us into persons who know in practice the hospitality you have extended to us. May we always make you welcome in return.

Teach Us to Pray

17th Sunday   C

Gn 18:20-32
Col 2:12-14
Lk 11:1-13

We are so quick to put the Lord on a pedestal. We are so impressed with the truth that he is God that we separate his experiences here on earth from ours. We so easily think of him as awesome and perhaps frightening because he was God walking among human beings. How else should a human being approach God except with awe?

And yet the Lord was God-made-man; he was as completely human as he was divine. He ate and slept, he cried and got tired, he learned and marvelled. He died. He did not awe people by walking among them as God; he walked among them as a man. They reacted to him as a man, even to the extent of thinking they could get rid of him by killing him—a standard response of society to a troublemaker, but hardly the standard response of a people to their God.

Lord, the most complete indication of how human you were is your prayer: the 40 days in the desert, the long nights during your teaching career, the terrifying prayer at Gethsemane, the agonized cry on the cross. You prayed because you needed to pray.

And, Lord, if *you* needed prayer, how can we convince ourselves that *we* can do without it? We look at our days, and we see a smattering of prayers morning and evening, before meals and at Sunday Mass. But we can forget prayer too easily. Even when you come to us in the Blessed Sacrament, our prayer stops short—and for such trivial reasons.

Lord, we need prayer so much more than you did. We are the dry wood on your Father's vine. And you are the green wood.

Lord, we ask: Make your Father a necessity in our lives. Make us aware of him and how much we need him. Open our eyes to our own littleness, and help us to raise our hearts and minds to God our Father. Lord, teach *us* to pray.

Give Us Your Peace Eccl 1:2; 2:21-23
Col 3:1-5, 9-11
18th Sunday   C Lk 12:13-21

The Lord sat on the hill opposite Jerusalem and wept. "O Jerusalem, Jerusalem. . . . How often have I yearned to gather your children, as a mother bird gathers her young under her wings, but you refused me" (Mt 23:37). And in the eternity of heaven he must still look out on this world and say exactly the same thing. He knows what is for our peace, and he wants to gather us together. We think we know better, and so we scatter after our own interests and for our own gains.

We think that we know what is for our own peace. We move from apartment to house to larger house; we work and scrimp and save. And the years go by. We have fallen in love with tomorrow, and we are never satisfied with today.

So where is our peace? The pursuit of the perfect home or the perfect job sometimes leaves us with the taste of ashes in our mouths. Even those of us who "have it made" still know in our hearts the emptiness of our pursuits. The blessings we have striven so hard to achieve don't bring the relaxation and peace we had wanted.

Lord, you are our peace. Your words are our peace. The love you have for us and that we have for one another: This is our peace. A heart that turns from sinful selfishness is our peace. A job well-done is our peace. Our peace is not in our gaining the whole world for ourselves. Our peace is in receiving you and all other persons in you.

Lord, give us *your* peace.

Valuing a Gift

19th Sunday C

Wis 18:6-9
Heb 11:1-2, 8-19
Lk 12:32-48

Today's Gospel speaks about our humdrum lives, speaks to us to remind us that our humdrum lives are much more than just that. The Lord's gift to us encompasses so much. It can take the kind of day we had yesterday or the day before and transform it by touching it with his presence and his love. Our lives at home and at work are not only *our* lives; they also belong to him. He wants to be a part of them now, just as he will be a part of them for eternity.

It is strange how we can so easily live our lives ignoring Jesus. It is not that we don't want him; we do. But remembering how much we planned for our last vacation and how the thought of it brightened the weeks before it, we can sometimes wonder why the thought of being with the Lord forever does not brighten our days while we wait.

For some people he still is important. He fills their days, and they do want him, even at some danger to themselves. Priests are dying in dungeons in South America and in work camps in Siberia because the Lord is important to them. And people gather for secret Eucharists in more than one modern atheistic country because the Lord means more to them than even their own lives.

Lord, we sometimes ask ourselves: "If we really had to struggle to find you and have you, would we bother?"

Maybe we would. We never know how valuable some things are until we see them disappearing. We remember the void left when someone we loved died or went away. We love you, Lord, and we want you. Help us, we ask you, to want you more deeply than we do now, and more consistently and persistently. You are our treasure; make us value you at your true worth. Don't allow us to remain blind to you today or ever.

Necessary Division   Jer 38:4-6, 8-10
                               Heb 12:1-4
20th Sunday   C   Lk 12:49-53

Sometimes we pride ourselves on our ability to get along with *anybody*. St. Paul seems to encourage us in our broadmindedness when he says: "I have made myself all things to all men" (1 Cor 9:22). For the sake of keeping peace in the family we will avoid topics that ignite arguments at the dinner table. Or, to be sure of our chances for promotion, we never disagree with the boss.

Maybe we have to act this way. We must provide for our family, and so what use is it to kill our chances for more money? And certainly an endless series of mealtime fights is not good for digestion. Yet we hear of Jeremiah today, and we wonder about our willingness to bow before every pressure that others exert against us.

Jeremiah stood like a rock against the opinions of the most important people in the country, and he would not bow even when they tried to kill him. And even Paul, despite his words to the Corinthians, argued with Peter, with his travelling companions, with the Pharisees, the Greeks and the Romans. He too had to face death from others. The words the Lord speaks in today's Gospel can frighten us. Does he really want our families to be divided within themselves?

Perhaps he would answer, "If every family accepts me and my word, no family will be divided against itself. I am of supreme importance to every family and to each member of the family. Division might come when one member accepts me and my values, and another does not. Even then there could be peace. Division will come when my follower follows me against the will of others. And that will sometimes happen."

So, Lord, we pray: Make me an instrument of your peace. But keep us from becoming so broadminded that false peace becomes more important than you yourself.

Asking the Right Questions

21st Sunday C

Is 66:18-21
Heb 12:5-7, 11-13
Lk 13:22-30

It is easy to ask the wrong questions. Once the apostles questioned the Lord about when the end of time would come. He told them it was not important for them to know. They had only to expect it and to live as if it would happen momentarily.

How many people are to be saved is equally unimportant. It would be idle to know whether heaven is to be populated with thousands or millions. The essential fact is that the Father wills that everyone be saved. If anyone is missing it will not be because God has gone down the line of people choosing some and rejecting others. He would not do that; no real father would.

If the number of the saved is small, it is because we have liked the broad and easy road better than the disciplined path the Father wants us to take. He never disinherits us; we abandon him.

Lord, let us ask the right questions. Let us wonder if we are generous and kind, if we are quick to forgive when we are hurt. Are we good parents and conscientious workers? Are we faithful in prayer?

These are the questions we need to ask. Let us trust you to answer the rest when the time is ripe.

With Open Arms

22nd Sunday C

Sir 3:17-18, 20, 28-29
Heb 12:18-19, 22-24
Lk 14:1, 7-14

We sometimes form the strangest images of Jesus. We can make him into somebody too distant to sit with at table or drink with at a wedding or walk with through a field of lilies. We can make him so awesome that we could never be comfortable with him. And as for the Father, our picture of him might amuse him. Michel-

angelo did not help us very much when he painted the
Father as a majestic bearded man touching a drowsy
Adam.

But the difference between Jesus and the Father is
that people did see Jesus. They ate with him, drank with
him, walked and talked and were friendly with him. He
was approachable. His most important job was to make
the invisible Father real to people. The Lord could do
that only if *he* were real to them.

That is why the image each one of us has of him is
so important. Part of that image should be the Jesus we
hear of in today's readings—a Jesus who has his arms
wide open inviting everyone, absolutely everyone, to
happiness now and forever. This Jesus reveals the invitation the Father extends to all people.

**Lord, you and your Father are so generous and
warm, loving and open. You don't want anyone to be
left out in the cold. All we must do is respond to your
invitation.**

**Lord, cleanse our image of you. Do not allow us to
make you into our image and likeness. Let us see you
and respond to you as you really are: open-armed,
human-hearted, inviting us to happiness, peace and joy.**

The Leap of Love

23rd Sunday   C

Wis 9:13-18
Phlm 9-10, 12-17
Lk 14:25-33

Today's readings invite us to a kind of prudence
not many of us know how to practice. When we think
of prudence, we usually have in mind a kind of cool
calculation that never allows us to begin something
whose consequences we can't foresee. Being prudent, we
think, means carefully avoiding all risk.

But the prudence to which the Lord invites us is
rather a willingness to know the risk we accept. It is the
prudence of lovers who pledge lifelong fidelity in a leap

into the unknown. When we marry, we promise our whole selves to another human being until the day we die, and we have no crystal ball to let us know what that promise really involves. When we say we will be true through riches and poverty, through sickness and health until death parts us, we stake our integrity on a scenario which unfolds in a day-by-day drama full of surprises.

It is just that leap of love the Lord asks of us today. He cautions that we must know the risk we take, the price we pay. The weight and shape of the cross we will carry on his path is not made clear; but his path *is* the way of the cross. The only guarantee he offers is that we will not walk alone; his footsteps will guide us.

Lord, you ask us to calculate the risk—but not to refuse it. We will not falter if we trust in you. We will falter only when, like Peter on the water, we forget you and think only of ourselves and our own safety.

Lord, the worst risk is to trust only in ourselves. Give us the courage to leap into the arms of a lover we cannot see. Give us the prudence to accept the risk of infinite love.

The Father Who Cannot Forget   Ex 32:7-11, 13-14
1 Tm 1:12-17
24th Sunday   C   Lk 15:1-32

Children bring their parents so much joy; but sometimes they make them suffer. Nothing causes more pain than when children repudiate their parents, slam the door and leave, saying in effect: "You are my mother and father no longer." The parental anguish is excruciating.

If such parents should open the door one morning and find their child sitting on the doorstep, or answer the phone and hear the familiar voice say, "Hi, Mom; hi, Dad," great joy would surge up in them. Bone of their bones and flesh of their flesh would make them whole again, and they would sweep the child into their arms and feel like having a party.

No wonder the Lord could find no better name to give to God than Father. The experiences we know as parents, he knows too. And why not? He made all of us in his image and likeness; and where are we more like him than in engendering new life, nurturing and loving it? And where are we more vulnerable than in our offspring's ingratitude and indifference—even hate? God goes through all this. In the first reading today we see his hurt and anger at the unfaithfulness of his people; and yet we also see how easily he can be turned from that hurt.

And in the Gospel Jesus tells the poignant story of the father who will not stand on his dignity and claim his rights; who will not demand an apology or punish; who will simply welcome his son home with an enthusiasm and a joy that infuriates the son's brother. But then the older son is not yet a father. Maybe his reactions would have been different if everything had happened 20 years later.

Lord Jesus, you urged us to become perfect like your Father. We have a head start with the parental love you have placed in our hearts. Don't allow us to ruin that love. Don't permit us to close ourselves to those who hurt us.

Open us, Lord, to that greatness of heart that knows no limits to its forgiveness and its power to welcome. And when we know the joy of using that love in our own homes and for our own children, guide us to its use for everyone. Help us to open our hearts to everyone, especially to those who have wounded us.

Justice or Profit?

25th Sunday   C

Am 8:4-7
1 Tm 2:1-8
Lk 16:1-13

We don't have to go far in our modern world to see some of the attitudes for which Amos rebuked the people of Israel. He condemned them for fraudulent business practices, for digging the last penny out of the powerless poor and for becoming impatient with any law and any person that hindered their money-making.

Today's money-making has more than just a nodding acquaintance with Amos' business world. We are offered carloads of contaminated wheat, automobiles with switched engines, shoddily-built homes, sleeping garments that can cause cancer, fresh cement that crumbles in a year or two—all in the sacred name of profit. It is difficult to find a product or a worker whose first quality is integrity.

We are in the middle of this kind of society. We produce for it, and we consume its products. We cannot divorce ourselves from it, not unless we go to the wilderness and eat what we capture or grow. Our problem is to discover how *much* we are a part of our culture. How strong a temptation it is for us to be conquered by it! We buy a new car, and even while it is in warranty, we come to the horrifying conclusion that it is a "lemon." Will we present the car to the next purchaser with a clear statement of its defects and take a financial loss? Or will we keep silent and hope we can pass the car off with a profit?

Lord, help us not to compromise between justice and profit. Make us trustworthy in all matters, large and small. Help us really to believe your word and act on it, even when it hurts.

Lazarus at Our Door　　　　　　　　Am 6:1, 4-7
　　　　　　　　　　　　　　　　　　　Tm 6:11-16
26th Sunday　C　　　　　　　　　　　Lk 16:19-31

Again the Lord echoes the prophets to make us uncomfortable with the luxuries we have made into necessities. Amos blasts the people who have it made. They are the ones who manipulated the trade practices of his day to make their fortunes. They now enjoy the luxuries that money can purchase. Amos berates them for their easy and indolent existence, their blindness to the world around them.

The story of the rich man and Lazarus presents the same kind of situation. The rich man enjoys what his money can buy and ignores the poor. And he is consigned to hell.

That judgment can be a shock to us who believe that only mortal sin sends anyone to hell. Where was the sin in the rich man's relationship with Lazarus? The rich man did not kill him, hit him, or get angry with him. He just ignored him.

Lord, is that enough for mortal sin? Is *not* doing something as much a sin as doing something? If we had our hearts and ears open, we would know your answer. You will judge us on our care for others.

Lord, help us to see Lazarus at our door. Help us to recognize him, care for him, and never think ourselves virtuous because we have not beaten him away with a broom. We are linked to him on our way to everlasting life. Let us treasure him.

Beyond Law　　　　　　　　　　　Hb 1:2-3; 2:2-4
　　　　　　　　　　　　　　　　　　2 Tm 1:6-8, 13-14
27th Sunday　C　　　　　　　　　　　Lk 17:5-10

We certainly know the commandments the Father proclaimed in the midst of fire on Mount Sinai. They were important to him, and they must be important to us, too. We know the commandments. We try to observe them, and we often find that observance difficult. So, when we go to confession, we feel pretty good when we can say to ourselves: "Not bad; nothing really serious this time."

And then we hear the Lord say: "When you have done all that you have been commanded to do, say, 'We are useless servants. We have done no more than our duty' " (Lk 17:10). That can hurt—especially when we realize that we have been congratulating ourselves for what we have *not* done, without considering all that we were supposed to do. What does the Lord want of us?

Well, it seems obvious that he wants us to go beyond avoiding sin. He wants us also to do and be *good*. Not only must we not want another woman badly enough to be willing to break up a marriage, we must do everything we can to protect and enrich every marriage we know. Not only must we keep our caustic tongues quiet, we must sweeten them with words of praise and encouragement. It means that our confessions reveal not only the evil we have done, but also the good we have not done.

Lord, help us to understand that we must pass beyond the limits of the law. Lead us into the freedom of the children of God, where sin is unthinkable and the love of God and others is our law.

Welcoming the Outcasts 2 Kgs 5:14-17
  2 Tm 2:8-13
28th Sunday   C Lk 17:11-19

We have often heard the story of the 10 lepers explained in terms of gratitude and ingratitude, and the explanation is a good one. To have that awful affliction healed is a gift that demands a "thank you." Perhaps we could never understand how completely such a cure would change our life unless we had cancer and were told one day, "It's remitted and we don't know why." One day, a sentence of death; the next, a birth to new life. It would be a fantastic experience, and we certainly would want to thank somebody.

For those 10 lepers, there was an even greater gift. Leprosy in Israel carried with it social consequences; to be a leper meant being an outcast. The leper was excluded from society and shunned even by family and friends. So a cure for the 10 lepers meant not only physical healing—it was literally a resurrection from the dead.

We can imagine the healed ones being welcomed back into their families and communities. And maybe that is where the other nine went—back to those who loved them. They forgot to say "thank you," but their excitement and joy are understandable.

Lord, who are the lepers among us? Who are the lonely, the outsiders, the ones who are unlike the rest of us? Who are the persons who are uncomfortable in a crowd or wallflowers at a party? Who are those so shy that they cannot have a good time at our parties and our dances? There are so many outcasts among us, so many afflicted with a sense of not belonging.

Lord, fill our hearts with your love so that we may extend our hands to those too shy to extend theirs. Let us do it with your gentleness and your kindness. If we are rebuffed, let us remember that you were, too. But let us never again participate in keeping anyone outside.

Increase Our Faith

29th Sunday   C

Ex 17:8-13
2 Tm 3:14—4:2
Lk 18:1-8

The Gospels often show the Lord at prayer. Once he prayed for so long a time that his body was weakened and he was subject to the visitations of an abominable evil. Sometimes he left everyone back in the town

while he wandered to a deserted place where he forgot
sleep and prayed to the Father until the sun rose. He
prayed at a supper table with a vehemence and a conviction that his listeners, the apostles, never forgot.
Once he prayed during a personal agony and a devastating fear that forced sweat like blood from his body. And
once he prayed in the midst of every circumstance that
could have invited him to succumb to Job's temptation:
"Curse God and die" (Jb 2:9b). He was pinned to a tree
with iron studs, bleeding and gasping for breath; he saw
hatred and triumph on the faces of those he had wanted
to gather into his love. He was alone up there. Still, he
prayed.

    Lord, what is it about prayer that you valued so
highly? Why did you pray so much, and why did you
urge us to pray ceaselessly? Is it because prayer and
faith are so closely related?
    **Prayer is the language of faith. Because we believe
that God is our Father, we speak to him as his children.
But when prayer is a rarity in our day, faith grows
scarce in our life. For faith is being ready to say yes to
the Father. Faith is the conviction that God is real—and
real to *us*.**
    Lord, we ask you to teach us prayer; we also ask,
"Help us grow in faith."

In One Big Bag Sir 35:12-14, 16-18
2 Tm 4:6-8, 16-18
30th Sunday   C Lk 18:9-14

    Why did the Lord condemn the Pharisee for his
prayer? Surely nothing can be wrong with fasting; Christ
himself fasted for 40 days when he began his career.
And where is the evil in tithing? If any pastor could
count on a 10th of every parishioner's earnings, he
would present his parish for collective canonization.
The Pharisee is merely pointing out his devotion to the

three great works of the Mosaic Law: prayer, fasting and almsgiving.

But that is exactly why he is condemned—for pointing them out. Activities that should have been a reaching out in humility towards God and neighbor had ceased to be that kind of activity for the Pharisee. He was no longer reaching out to anyone. His prayer, fasting and almsgiving were not done for others; they were done for himself. And so he was condemned, even though he was giving a penny on every dime, a dime on every dollar. He was paying a high price, indeed, for the Lord's disapproval.

And the Lord praised the hated tax-gatherer for *his* prayer. Not only was he no giver of tithes; he was an avid extortioner. Something must have happened to him to make him realize that his injustice to others was sin, because that is what he was now calling himself: a sinner. His prayer reached out to a forgiving Father; when he left the temple, he would be expected to reach out to the brothers and sisters he had wronged.

Lord, teach us to realize that prayer, sincerity, justice and our Father, our brothers and sisters are all bound up in one big bag. Help us to be convinced that we can't have one without the others.

An Enthusiastic Welcome   Wis 11:22—12:1
2 Thes 1:11—2:2
31st Sunday   C   Lk 19:1-10

Zacchaeus may be one of the most attractive people in the New Testament. But he was not always very lovable. He was a tax collector, enriching himself and the Romans at the expense of his own fellow-Jews. No wonder then that the other Jews were scandalized when the Lord went to dine at Zacchaeus' house. Luke says that *everyone* murmured.

They were right. Zacchaeus *was* a sinner, a bad one.

But when Jesus happened along, Zacchaeus looked at him and at himself—and changed. The really lovable thing about him was his enthusiasm for meeting the Lord. A little man, a "runt," he sprinted past the crowd that surrounded Jesus and climbed a tree so that he could see. What a picture—this rich, influential worldling perched on a tree limb!

The Lord was wonderful with him and he responded beautifully. Zacchaeus became the Lord's host. He said goodbye to sin and extortion and promised to pay back four times over whatever he had extorted.

Lord, have you seen Zacchaeus in our church? Did we run to see you and to be with you? Do you hear us saying to you at the moment of sacramental union: "Lord, whatever wrong I have done I will correct at no matter what cost to me?"

Lord, you have made each one of us your host; you are our guest. We pray to you, Lord: Give us a heart complete in your service. Make us forget embarrassment in opening ourselves to you. Bring us to that simplicity of Zacchaeus so that our past sins and their profits will no longer keep us from you. Make each of us into a real Zacchaeus.

The Defeat of Death

32nd Sunday   C

2 Mc 7:1-2, 9-14
2 Thes 2:16—3:5
Lk 20:27-38

The first reading and Gospel of today are an invitation to take a close look at the fact of death.

In the last centuries of the Old Testament men and women were sensing that death was not a cessation of all life. They were beginning to see it as a transition to new life. This insight could make suffering even something as severe as martyrdom worthwhile.

This is the whole point behind today's story of the Maccabees. And it is what lies behind Jesus' almost contemptuous answer to the Sadducees' silly and contentious question in today's Gospel. They were materialistic men with no belief in life after death, even though many of their own people had come to cherish that belief after centuries of reflection.

For Jesus, that belief was everything. It lay beneath his promise to us of everlasting life, and beneath his own last cry on the cross when he commended his spirit to the Father.

Jesus sensed that his death would reveal his unswerving loyalty to the Father, a loyalty that Scripture praises when it says that Jesus was obedient unto death, the shameful death on the cross. He knew, too, that his Father would respond to that loyalty with the gift of a life that would never again bow to the last great enemy. Jesus' death destroyed death, and we are all the gainers.

Lord Jesus, make our belief in everlasting life with you vital and productive in our lives. Even in our fear of death, give us the confidence of life. And when the moment comes for each one of us, listen to your mother as she prays for us "now and at the hour of our death." You, Lord, defeated death. Make your victory ours.

An Unlimited Horizon

Mal 3:19-20
2 Thes 3:7-12
Lk 21:5-19

33rd Sunday   C

We work at building our lives. We have invested ourselves heavily in our homes, our families, our jobs, our town, our parish. Our lives are for each of us "a time to build" (Eccl 3:3b). For so many of us, that time is now.

But time works its inevitable way on our bodies. Our mirrors tell us that building cannot go on forever. Our faces get lined and dry, our bodies weaken, our steps slow. Young lives grow up around us, only to leave and build lives of their own. We are also living witnesses to the reality that there is "a time to tear down" (Eccl 3:3b). Like it or not, we know our building must end.

All of us, no matter where we are in our life's pilgrimage to the Lord, must try to understand the limited horizon within which our earthly work is done. It is good that we work, and sweat is no mark of dishonor; it is good that we build for as long as we can. But we must try to realize that our work, our home, our family can create a horizon that is much too narrow and that can hide another horizon as wide as God himself.

Lord, you came to show us a vision beyond our life and our death. It is a vision of life that never ends. Begun at Baptism, it is lived in and through and beyond our 60 or 80 years on this earth. It is a life you give us every moment of our lives. You ask that we see it as our true life and, in its light, gauge every value that we pursue. Lord, you did not create us only for this world. You created us so that in and by this world, we may know you now and always.

Lord, you warn us that what we have built here will not stand. Help us to think about that. It is a wise and sobering thought—and not necessarily a pessimistic one.

Absolute Fullness

2 Sm 5:1-3
Col 1:12-20
Lk 23:35-43

34th or Last Sunday of the Year
Christ the King   C

Here at the end of the Church year we are invited to make a final act of faith in the Lord and what he has done for us. For 52 weeks we have come to Mass and have offered ourselves to the Father through him, and shared his gift of bread and wine. We have prayed and promised that our week-to-come would be more worthy of him. Sundays are supposed to be the most important days of the week; meeting the Lord in word and sacrament is supposed to be the most important thing we do on Sunday. From that meeting comes all that makes the rest of the week a joyful and blessed living. Indeed, he is at the center of our Sundays, our weeks and our lives.

And that is what this Sunday, this feast of Christ the King, is all about. It is a chance for us to reflect on the center of all creation and to see whether we have allowed the Lord to be shifted away from our own center to some position on the periphery of what we hold important. Sometimes honesty forces us to say that he has not always been to us the absolute fullness Paul describes.

To be a Christian wife or husband is to be something different from being *merely* a wife or husband. A Christian home is different from one where the Lord is unknown. A job is different when governed by Christian principles rather than pagan ones.

Lord, you either make a difference in our lives or you do not. Here at the end of the year, we must admit that you have *not* always and everywhere been our fullness. But we thank you for those times when the clouds of our selfishness and our laziness parted, and we could see your presence a bit more clearly. You are always there; all we have to do is to open our eyes.

Lord, at the end of this Church year we say again that you are our salvation, our hope, our glory. Shake us into awareness of you. Lord, increase our faith!

Holydays and Holidays

An Important Person Gn 3:9-15, 20
 Eph 1:3-6, 11-12
Immaculate Conception Lk 1:26-38

Because the Lord promises to be with the Church until the end of time, because he really made us one with him, Mary is honored by the Church. The Church throughout its history has treated Mary the way Jesus would have treated her. And the Church has tried hard to treat her well. Some of the loveliest hymns we sing are to her, and some of the Church's most tender feasts are about her. The Church is fascinated by Mary and expresses its love in a chaplet of beautiful names: Mystical Rose, Tower of Ivory, Ark of the Covenant. Mary has always been important to us. She is important to us because the Lord is important to us.

For Christ and Mary are linked together by a bond that always includes us too. Maybe that is why our strong instinct is to turn to her. Maybe, too, that is why when a generation forgets her, it starts to forget him also. Her prediction that *all* generations would call her "blessed" was no sign of pride. She knew that all her blessedness came from the Lord. And we know that her blessedness was a whole series of favors that came to her because she was the first one among us to feel the effects of his saving power.

Lord, Mary is for us the example of what you want your world to be: sinless, open to your Father, and with you and your Father forever. She is the first to be saved, our guarantee that you, the firstfruits, are already joined by the rest of the harvest.

Lord, let us never allow Mary to slip out of our prayer. Let us understand how important she always is to us. Because when we forget her, we also forget the monumental importance of your gifts to her of sinlessness and bodily resurrection. We forget the awfulness of sin and the glory of heaven. In other words, Lord, we forget what you are all about when we forget what you did for her. Let us never be that foolish, Lord!

Everyday Saints   Rv 7:2-4, 9-14
                            1 Jn 3:1-3
All Saints   Mt 5:1-12

All during the year we have celebrated the feasts of the great ones of the Church. They are an astonishing set of people, the heroes and heroines who said yes to the Lord so resoundingly. These are the men and women in every generation through whom God says to all the rest of us: "This is what I'm talking about. They were men and women like you. If they can do it, so can you. Maybe not as spectacularly, but what they were in their hearts, you can be."

So today we celebrate all those other people whose hearts have been open to the Lord, but whose lives were known only to a few. Today we celebrate the mothers whose whole lives were an act of love for the children, and the fathers whose one concern was the careful nurturing of their family. We celebrate the workmen who gave their best, and the businessmen and women who dealt with humanity with honesty and justice. We celebrate the doctors whose care for their patients was touched by compassion, and the kindly neighbors who were always there in time of trouble. We celebrate today those millions who lived their lives in goodness and who died in the peace of single-hearted love.

All of these people, Lord, went before us in the same paths we tread daily, and they are saints. We don't know their names—at least not all of them. We each could make a little litany of good people whose lives have been a blessing to us. We remember them today and thank you for their presence among us.

Today too, Lord, we remember ourselves, and we ask you that we may live out our lives in the simple goodness you want of us. You have assured us—we *can* be saints.

The Birth of a Mother

The Assumption

Rv 11:19; 12:1-6, 10
1 Cor 15:20-26
Lk 1:39-56

We thank the Lord for the gift of his mother to us from the cross. It was an astonishing reversal of roles. Usually the mother brings forth her child in pain and anguish and essential loneliness. But on the cross Jesus, in suffering and abandonment, brought a mother into the family he was creating.

His whole message was that *his* Father is ours too; and that we are brothers and sisters to each other and to the Lord. The only person missing in the family circle was a mother—and he gave us one in Mary.

Today's feast can be so reassuring to all of us. It is a pledge to us that the family is already constituted in heaven waiting until all its members are gathered together around the eternal table. The Father raised Jesus from the dead as the firstborn of the family; and then brought Mary to join him. Now Father and Son and mother wait for the rest of us to come home from our different journeys so that our joy can be made perfect in the Spirit's unity of divine love. Mary is the first ingathering of the Lord's harvest.

Lord, all of us still on this earth are indeed on journeys. We are subject to so many foolish diversions on our way home. Some of us play the prodigal. Many of us set up an earthly home that we mistake for the

end of our trip. But no place here can be the end of our trip, Lord. You made our longing hearts too deep to fool ourselves perpetually with that delusion, and in our saner moments we realize it. You made us for heaven.

Lord, on this feast of your giving Mary her motherly place in heaven, give us too a conscious and profound desire to be with you and the Father and her. Make us want heaven. And listen to your mother as she prays to you for each of us, her children. She always prays for us now and at the hour of our death. After all, she is our mother.

A Mother's Love

Mother's Day

We have seen Michelangelo's statue of Mary receiving Christ's lifeless body from the cross and resting it across her lap. The statue is a companion portrait to Mary cradling him as an infant, her whole life one vast expectation. Any mother who holds her baby for the first time knows Mary's emotions and hopes when she first fondled her son. But Michaelangelo's statue shows the last touch. Mary's hopes had ended on a cross. Her son was dead. Now she knows only resignation. But even as she holds the Lord in death, her relationship has not changed. She is close to him; she touches him; she loves him. And she waits.

Mary is the image of all mothers. Only they know the pain we cause them when we first enter the world. And only they know the hopes that surge within their hearts as they hold us for the first time and forecast a life closed to no success. But we know that we have hardly lived up to their hopes. We know the disappointments we have caused them, the agony we have sometimes stirred in their hearts. Mothers always seem to be waiting; their children are never completed. Always, we think, a mother senses other possibilities—sometimes bad, sometimes good—for her child.

At times, Lord, that sense of waiting for us to be what we are not already oppresses us. We think that we can never satisfy our mothers. But, Lord, we can be so wrong in that judgment. Most of our mothers are like Mary; they wait and hope and expect—but in the end they accept what we make of ourselves. And if we ascend a cross, they accept even that, allowing their suffering to endure when ours is over.

Lord Jesus, a mother's love is not something to get sentimental about. It is something to try to understand and to treasure. It is a rare and lovely thing. Today we salute it and the women in whose hearts it dwells. Lord Jesus, we thank you for our mothers.

In the Image of the Father

Father's Day

Each one of us brings personal memories to today's celebration of Father's Day. Each one comes from a different background, and each one knows a father in a way unlike anyone else. Even if our family was large, each one of us came into the family in a different place in the sequence; we knew our father as he was during our own particular time of growing up. The oldest remember a young man whom they saw age; the youngest may remember him as always middle-aged and older. In any case, our father holds a unique place in our lives.

How do we remember our father? As kindly and gentle, loving and firm? Was he the kind of man who thought first of our needs and only then—if ever—of his own? Was he the one who taught us, more by his actions than by his words, that fairness and honesty were important? Or was he a brutal and willful tyrant whom we feared and tried to stay away from? Or a man whom we knew only fleetingly because he was so seldom at home?

Or a person whom we only sensed through the loving memory of our mother because the Lord, for whatever reason, brought him home to himself before we had a chance to know him?

Lord, our father is so important to us because our memories of him are the basis for our concept of your Father. We can know so much about your Father by thinking about ours. You made it that way. You taught us to call God our Father because you knew intimately his fatherly love.

So, Lord, if our father was a gentle, kind and firm man, we thank you. You have given us an invaluable gift. And we who are now fathers thank you, because you invite us to share in the deepest impulses of a God who is, above all things else, a Father. Help us, Lord, to be like him.

The Gift of Our Country

Thanksgiving

This day means so much to us Americans! We don't want to make a god of our country or a religion of our patriotism, but we do think that the Lord has been extraordinarily generous to us in this land. A trip through any part of this country opens before us the pages of a great love letter God has written, not in words, but in terrain.

We treasure the heritage of liberty into which we have been born. We see there a sign of the divine courtesy with which the Lord treats us. He forces no one. He asks and he waits for an answer. He instructs and he urges, but the very essence of the response he awaits is freedom. His kingdom is a place of freedom where, without force or coercion, everyone is what he or she most perfectly wants to be. Our national heritage reflects the image of that personal freedom. We have made some hideous mistakes in our pursuit of liberty and justice for all. But then, our country is not heaven.

We think, Lord, about the freedom with which we have gathered to thank you here today. Some countries would never think of a national day of giving thanks to you. Others would not permit it. But here we glory in the churches that dot our landscape and in the peace we allow one another to gather in groups before you. We have made mistakes even in this intimate area; but the freedom is more evident than the mistakes, and for this we are grateful.

Lord, we thank you deeply and sincerely today for your gifts to us and to our country. Help us to respect our freedoms, the earth and all its goodness, the beauty you have spread so lavishly about. You have given all of it.